Advanced Capital Markets Strategy for Business Owners

How to Build Multiple Exit Paths, Increase Valuation, and Maximize Long-Term Wealth

By Joe Correa

Published by Live Stronger Faster

This book is for educational and informational purposes only. The author and publisher are not engaged in rendering legal, financial, or other professional advice. Readers should consult a qualified professional before making any financial decisions.

First Edition

Table of Contents

Introduction 5

Chapter 1: Understanding Advanced Capital Markets and the New Rules of Wealth Creation....15

Chapter 2: Building Multiple Exit Paths and Maximizing Strategic Optionality....32

Chapter 3: Increasing Company Valuation Through Scalability, Positioning, and Investor Psychology....50

Chapter 4: Institutional Investors, Private Equity, and the Mechanics of Large-Scale Capital....68

Chapter 5: Timing the Market, Economic Cycles, and the Psychology of Capital Flows....86

Chapter 6: IPOs, Acquisitions, and Designing the Perfect Exit Strategy....104

Chapter 7: Building Generational Wealth Through Equity, Ownership, and Long-Term Capital Allocation....121

Chapter 8: The Future of Capital Markets, AI, and the Next Generation of Wealth Creation....137

Chapter 9: Building an Empire Mindset – From Entrepreneur to Capital Allocator....154

Chapter 10: The Billion-Dollar Framework – Scaling Beyond the Founder....169

Final IPO Thoughts....185

Introduction

The journey from private business ownership to long-term wealth creation through capital markets represents one of the most transformative financial opportunities available to entrepreneurs. While many business owners focus primarily on generating income, maintaining operations, or expanding market share, relatively few fully understand how advanced capital markets strategies can dramatically multiply both company valuation and personal net worth over time. The difference between a business owner who simply operates a successful company and one who strategically builds an enterprise designed for liquidity, scalability, and multiple exit opportunities can amount to tens of millions—or even billions—of dollars in long-term wealth creation. This book was created to help business owners, founders, investors, and entrepreneurs understand how sophisticated capital markets strategies work and how these strategies can be used to maximize enterprise value while simultaneously building financial freedom and generational wealth.

Throughout history, some of the world's wealthiest individuals did not simply earn high incomes. Instead, they built equity in scalable businesses, positioned those companies strategically within the marketplace, and eventually converted ownership into liquidity through carefully engineered capital events. Whether through initial public offerings, mergers, acquisitions, direct listings, SPAC transactions, private equity recapitalizations, secondary sales, or long-term dividend strategies, the most successful entrepreneurs understand that wealth is often created not through salary but through ownership, leverage, timing, and strategic exits. Advanced capital markets strategy involves learning how to create multiple opportunities for liquidity while maintaining flexibility and control over the direction of the business.

One of the most important concepts in modern business wealth creation is optionality. Sophisticated founders rarely rely on a single exit plan. Instead, they intentionally structure their businesses to support multiple pathways to liquidity and growth. A company may initially plan for a traditional IPO, but market conditions could later favor a SPAC merger, private equity acquisition, strategic buyout, or direct listing. Some companies may remain private while conducting secondary share sales that allow founders and early employees to create liquidity without giving up operational control. Other companies may use debt markets, convertible notes, or strategic partnerships to fuel expansion while postponing dilution. The founders who understand capital markets deeply are able to pivot intelligently between opportunities as market conditions evolve. The ability to create multiple exit paths is one of the defining characteristics of elite business strategy. Business owners who rely exclusively on one future outcome often place themselves in a vulnerable position. For example, if a founder builds a company solely for acquisition by a larger corporation, the entire strategy may collapse if acquisition markets weaken. Similarly, companies that rush toward IPOs without understanding broader market cycles may encounter severe valuation declines, liquidity problems, or shareholder dissatisfaction after going public. By contrast, companies that maintain strategic flexibility can adapt to changing economic conditions while preserving long-term value creation opportunities.

Advanced capital markets strategy begins long before any public transaction occurs. It starts with how a business is structured during its early and growth phases. Decisions related to ownership structure, governance, financial reporting, scalability, intellectual property, recurring revenue models, operational efficiency, legal compliance, and investor relations all play critical roles in determining how valuable a company becomes in the eyes of future investors or acquirers. Many founders mistakenly believe that valuation is determined only by revenue growth, but sophisticated capital markets participants evaluate companies based on many additional factors, including predictability of earnings, scalability of operations, defensibility of market position, customer retention, management quality, technological advantages, and long-term expansion potential.

One of the most powerful concepts explored in this book is the relationship between scalability and valuation multiples. Businesses that rely heavily on the founder's personal labor or constant direct involvement often receive lower valuations because growth becomes difficult to sustain without the founder's continuous participation. In contrast, businesses with scalable systems, recurring revenue, automated infrastructure, strong management teams, intellectual property protection, and predictable cash flow often command significantly higher valuation multiples. Capital markets reward scalability because scalable businesses can grow rapidly without proportional increases in operational costs.

As companies mature, founders must begin thinking not only like operators but also like institutional investors. Institutional capital evaluates businesses through a completely different lens than most small business owners. Investors want to understand market opportunity size, customer acquisition economics, retention metrics, gross margins, operating leverage, expansion opportunities, competitive barriers, and long-term strategic positioning. Companies that learn how to communicate effectively with institutional investors often gain access to substantially larger pools of capital, which can accelerate growth dramatically. However, access to capital also introduces new responsibilities related to governance, transparency, shareholder expectations, and performance accountability.

Another major focus of advanced capital markets strategy involves understanding the timing of liquidity events. Timing plays a critical role in maximizing both valuation and long-term wealth preservation. Economic cycles, interest rates, investor sentiment, industry momentum, geopolitical conditions, and public market performance can all significantly influence valuation outcomes. Some founders destroy long-term value by attempting to exit too early, while others wait too long and miss optimal market windows. The ability to recognize favorable market conditions and align company readiness with capital market demand is one of the most valuable skills an entrepreneur can develop.

This book also explores how founders can preserve and protect wealth after liquidity events occur. Many entrepreneurs spend years building substantial equity only to lose significant portions of their wealth due to poor diversification strategies, excessive concentration risk, emotional decision-making, tax inefficiencies, or lack of long-term planning. Wealth creation and wealth preservation are not the same skill set. The transition from entrepreneur to high-net-worth individual requires a completely different approach to financial management, risk analysis, and strategic planning.

For many founders, going public or completing a major exit represents only the beginning of a much larger financial journey. Public equity can become a tool for future acquisitions, capital raising, expansion into international markets, or launching entirely new ventures. Public companies can leverage their stock as currency for mergers and strategic partnerships. Founders with significant public equity holdings may also gain access to lending strategies, family office structures, private investment opportunities, and advanced estate planning solutions that further compound long-term wealth. Understanding how to use equity strategically after liquidity events can create entirely new layers of financial opportunity.

Another important subject addressed throughout this book is dilution management. Raising capital often requires founders to exchange ownership for growth financing, but excessive dilution can significantly reduce long-term founder wealth. Advanced capital markets strategy involves balancing growth acceleration with ownership preservation. Some founders maintain strong control through dual-class share structures, strategic voting agreements, staged fundraising, or disciplined capital allocation strategies. Others intentionally dilute ownership in exchange for strategic partnerships or institutional credibility that substantially increases overall company value. Understanding when dilution creates value—and when it destroys value—is essential for long-term success.

Modern capital markets also reward narrative positioning and market perception. Companies are not valued solely based on numbers; they are often valued based on future expectations and market confidence. The ability to communicate a compelling growth narrative can significantly influence investor demand, valuation multiples, and market enthusiasm. This is why branding, leadership credibility, investor communication, public relations, and strategic storytelling play critical roles in advanced capital markets strategy. Investors often place enormous value on visionary leadership teams that can articulate scalable futures supported by strong operational execution.

As technology continues transforming global markets, new opportunities for capital formation are emerging rapidly. Artificial intelligence, fintech, blockchain infrastructure, creator economies, digital education, subscription platforms, and online business ecosystems have dramatically reduced barriers to scalability for entrepreneurs around the world. Businesses that once required enormous infrastructure investments can now achieve massive global reach using lean digital operating models. This shift has created unprecedented opportunities for founders to build highly scalable enterprises capable of generating significant enterprise value with relatively low overhead.

The democratization of entrepreneurship has also increased competition dramatically. As more companies enter the market, strategic positioning becomes increasingly important. Businesses must differentiate themselves not only through products and services but also through operational excellence, intellectual property, customer experience, strategic partnerships, and financial sophistication. Founders who understand advanced capital markets strategy gain a competitive advantage because they learn how to position their businesses in ways that attract institutional capital, strategic buyers, and long-term investor interest.

This book was designed to serve both aspiring entrepreneurs and experienced business owners who want to think at a much higher strategic level. Some readers may currently operate small private companies with ambitions of scaling nationally or globally. Others may already manage multimillion-dollar businesses and seek advanced strategies for maximizing valuation and planning future liquidity events. Regardless of where you currently stand in your entrepreneurial journey, understanding capital markets can fundamentally transform the way you think about business growth, ownership, and long-term wealth creation. You will learn how sophisticated founders engineer multiple exit opportunities rather than depending on a single outcome. You will explore how valuation psychology influences investor behavior and how business structure affects enterprise value. You will discover how timing, market cycles, and strategic positioning shape liquidity opportunities. Most importantly, you will begin thinking like both an entrepreneur and a capital allocator simultaneously—a combination that often separates ordinary business owners from extraordinary wealth creators.

The modern economy increasingly rewards ownership, scalability, intellectual property, and strategic leverage. Business owners who learn how to align their companies with capital markets gain access to opportunities that extend far beyond traditional income generation. They gain the ability to build enterprises that create wealth not only for themselves but also for employees, investors, communities, and future generations. The ultimate goal is not simply to build a profitable business. The ultimate goal is to build a scalable, valuable, adaptable enterprise capable of creating long-term financial freedom and enduring legacy.

As you move through this book, remember that advanced capital markets strategy is not reserved exclusively for billion-dollar corporations or elite Wall Street institutions. Many of the principles explored in these chapters can be applied by entrepreneurs at various stages of growth. Whether your company generates six figures, seven figures, or hundreds of millions in annual revenue, the ability to understand valuation, liquidity, ownership structure, investor psychology, and strategic exits can dramatically alter your long-term financial trajectory.

The future belongs to entrepreneurs who combine innovation with financial intelligence. It belongs to founders who understand how to scale businesses strategically while preserving ownership and maximizing flexibility. It belongs to leaders who recognize that wealth is created not only through operational execution but also through intelligent positioning within the broader capital markets ecosystem. This book is your guide to understanding that ecosystem and using it to build extraordinary long-term wealth.

Chapter 1

Understanding Advanced Capital Markets and the New Rules of Wealth Creation

The modern business world has evolved far beyond the traditional idea of simply owning a profitable company. In previous generations, many business owners focused almost entirely on generating revenue, maintaining operations, and producing consistent income. While profitability remains essential, today's most successful entrepreneurs understand that true wealth is often created not through annual income alone, but through ownership structures, enterprise valuation growth, strategic financing, liquidity planning, and intelligent participation in the capital markets ecosystem. Advanced capital markets strategy represents the intersection between entrepreneurship, finance, valuation engineering, investor psychology, and long-term wealth creation. Understanding how these systems work allows business owners to transform ordinary businesses into scalable financial assets capable of generating life-changing wealth.

Capital markets are the financial systems that connect businesses with investors seeking opportunities for growth and returns. These markets include public stock exchanges, private equity firms, venture capital funds, debt markets, institutional investors, hedge funds, family offices, and investment banks. While many small business owners believe these systems are reserved for massive corporations, the reality is that nearly every business eventually interacts with capital markets in some form. Whether a company raises outside funding, obtains debt financing, conducts a merger, sells equity, issues stock options, pursues acquisition opportunities, or eventually goes public, it becomes part of the broader capital markets environment.

One of the most important shifts entrepreneurs must make is learning to view their businesses not only as income-producing entities but also as financial assets. A company with strong systems, recurring revenue, intellectual property, operational efficiency, scalable infrastructure, and predictable growth may become extremely valuable even if the founder is not taking a large personal salary. Sophisticated investors focus heavily on future scalability and long-term cash flow potential rather than simply current owner income. This distinction changes how businesses are built, managed, and positioned for future growth.

Many entrepreneurs unknowingly limit the valuation potential of their businesses because they operate without scalable systems. Businesses that rely entirely on the founder's direct labor, personal relationships, or daily supervision often become difficult to scale. Investors and acquirers generally avoid companies that collapse without the founder's constant involvement. This is why advanced capital markets strategy places tremendous emphasis on building systems, delegation structures, automation, recurring revenue models, management teams, operational transparency, and institutional-level reporting. The more independent the business becomes from the founder personally, the more valuable the company may become in the eyes of institutional investors.

Another major principle of advanced capital markets strategy is understanding valuation multiples. Businesses are rarely sold or valued based solely on annual profit. Instead, investors often assign valuation multiples based on growth potential, scalability, industry positioning, competitive advantages, market opportunity, recurring revenue quality, and future earnings expectations. For example, two companies generating the exact same annual profit may receive dramatically different valuations depending on how investors perceive future growth potential. A local service business dependent on one owner may receive a relatively small multiple, while a scalable technology-enabled platform with recurring subscription revenue could receive an exponentially higher valuation despite producing similar current profits. This reality changes how strategic founders think about business operations. Rather than focusing only on short-term income extraction, sophisticated entrepreneurs often reinvest aggressively into growth, technology, marketing systems, management infrastructure, and intellectual property development. They understand that increasing enterprise value can ultimately create much larger wealth opportunities than maximizing annual distributions. Many founders who later achieve enormous liquidity events spent years sacrificing personal income in order to build scalable enterprise value.

The relationship between scalability and valuation becomes even more important as businesses approach institutional investment opportunities. Institutional investors seek companies capable of sustained growth without proportional increases in operational costs. Businesses with scalable operating models often achieve expanding profit margins as revenue grows. Software companies, subscription businesses, digital platforms, AI-driven businesses, online education companies, and technology-enabled financial platforms are prime examples of models that can scale globally without massive increases in labor costs. This scalability dramatically increases investor interest and valuation potential.

In advanced capital markets strategy, perception also plays a major role. Markets are heavily influenced by confidence, narrative, leadership credibility, and future expectations. Founders who understand investor psychology learn how to position their companies strategically within larger market trends. Investors often reward companies that align with growing industries, disruptive technologies, demographic shifts, or emerging consumer behaviors. The ability to communicate a compelling future vision can significantly influence both fundraising opportunities and valuation multiples.

Many successful public companies initially generated little or no profit during their growth stages. Investors continued funding these businesses because they believed in the long-term scalability of the underlying business models. This demonstrates one of the most important lessons in capital markets: future expectations often drive valuation more than present conditions. Business owners who understand this principle begin focusing heavily on strategic positioning, growth narratives, recurring revenue systems, customer acquisition scalability, and long-term expansion opportunities.

Another critical component of advanced capital markets strategy involves understanding the different stages of corporate growth financing. Businesses generally progress through several funding phases as they scale. Early-stage businesses may rely on personal savings, friends and family capital, or small angel investors. As companies grow, they may pursue venture capital, private equity financing, institutional debt facilities, mezzanine financing, or strategic partnerships. Mature companies may eventually access public equity markets through IPOs, direct listings, SPAC mergers, or secondary offerings. Each stage introduces different opportunities, risks, and ownership implications.

Ownership dilution is one of the most misunderstood concepts among entrepreneurs. Raising outside capital often requires founders to exchange portions of ownership for financing. While dilution reduces ownership percentage, it can substantially increase the overall value of the company if the capital accelerates growth successfully. For example, owning 100% of a $1 million company may ultimately produce less wealth than owning 30% of a $500 million company. Sophisticated founders learn how to evaluate dilution strategically rather than emotionally.

However, uncontrolled dilution can become dangerous. Many founders lose operational control or significantly reduce long-term wealth potential by raising capital inefficiently. Advanced capital markets strategy requires careful planning around fundraising structure, investor rights, voting control, liquidation preferences, board governance, and long-term ownership preservation. Some founders implement dual-class share structures that allow them to retain voting control despite reduced economic ownership. Others negotiate protective provisions that maintain strategic flexibility during future financing rounds.

Debt markets also play a major role in advanced capital markets strategy. Many entrepreneurs focus only on equity financing while underestimating the power of intelligent leverage. Debt financing allows businesses to access growth capital without immediately diluting ownership. However, leverage introduces financial risk and requires disciplined cash flow management. Sophisticated founders learn how to balance debt and equity strategically based on growth objectives, market conditions, and operational stability.

Public markets introduce entirely new dimensions of opportunity and complexity. Once companies become publicly traded, they gain access to significantly larger pools of capital. Public equity can be used for acquisitions, expansion initiatives, strategic partnerships, employee compensation programs, and institutional credibility enhancement. Publicly traded companies may also experience substantial increases in brand visibility, market influence, and investor interest.

At the same time, public markets create new responsibilities. Public companies must comply with extensive regulatory reporting requirements, shareholder expectations, quarterly earnings scrutiny, governance standards, and public transparency obligations. Some founders struggle emotionally with the transition from private control to public accountability. Advanced capital markets strategy therefore requires not only financial sophistication but also emotional discipline and long-term strategic thinking.

Market timing represents another essential factor in capital markets success. Economic cycles dramatically influence investor sentiment, valuation multiples, financing conditions, and liquidity opportunities. During bullish market environments, investors often reward growth aggressively and provide abundant capital access. During economic downturns, capital becomes more restrictive, valuations contract, and risk tolerance declines. Founders who understand macroeconomic cycles can position their businesses strategically to maximize opportunities during favorable market windows.

Interest rates also affect valuation dynamics significantly. Lower interest rate environments often increase investor appetite for growth assets because future earnings become more attractive relative to fixed-income alternatives. Higher interest rates generally compress valuation multiples and increase financing costs. Sophisticated entrepreneurs monitor these macroeconomic conditions carefully because they directly influence exit timing, fundraising opportunities, and acquisition activity.

One of the most powerful wealth-building concepts in advanced capital markets strategy is optionality. Optionality refers to maintaining multiple future strategic pathways rather than depending entirely on one outcome. Companies that preserve flexibility may pursue IPOs, acquisitions, private equity recapitalizations, secondary liquidity events, strategic partnerships, or continued private ownership depending on market conditions. Businesses with strong optionality typically command higher valuations because investors recognize their adaptability and strategic positioning.

Founders who understand optionality avoid becoming trapped by rigid business models or narrow exit expectations. Instead, they intentionally structure businesses to remain attractive under multiple future scenarios. This flexibility can significantly increase negotiating power during acquisition discussions or financing events because the company is not desperate for any single outcome.

Another important principle involves understanding liquidity planning. Many entrepreneurs focus exclusively on building enterprise value without considering how or when that value will eventually convert into personal financial liquidity. A founder may theoretically own a company worth hundreds of millions of dollars while remaining personally cash constrained. Advanced capital markets strategy requires planning around liquidity timelines, secondary sales, tax optimization, diversification, estate planning, and wealth preservation.

Taxes represent one of the largest long-term threats to wealth accumulation. Sophisticated founders work closely with tax advisors, estate attorneys, investment professionals, and wealth strategists to structure transactions intelligently. Capital gains planning, trust structures, charitable giving strategies, family offices, and geographic tax considerations can dramatically influence how much wealth founders ultimately retain after liquidity events occur.

The rise of global technology platforms has expanded opportunities for entrepreneurs dramatically. Modern businesses can now scale internationally using digital infrastructure, remote teams, AI automation, cloud computing, social media marketing, subscription models, and online education systems. Businesses that once required massive infrastructure investments can now reach global audiences with relatively lean operating costs. This shift has accelerated the creation of scalable business models capable of attracting institutional capital much earlier than in previous generations. Artificial intelligence and automation are now reshaping the future of capital markets as well. Investors increasingly seek businesses capable of leveraging AI for operational efficiency, customer acquisition, personalization, data analytics, and scalable automation. Companies that integrate advanced technologies effectively may achieve significantly higher operating leverage and long-term valuation potential.

Ultimately, advanced capital markets strategy is about understanding how financial systems reward scalability, predictability, growth, positioning, and strategic flexibility. The entrepreneurs who create the greatest long-term wealth are rarely those who simply work the hardest. Instead, they are often the individuals who learn how to structure businesses intelligently, position companies strategically, leverage capital effectively, preserve ownership carefully, and align their enterprises with long-term investor demand.

As you continue through this book, you will begin thinking beyond ordinary business ownership. You will start viewing your company as a scalable financial asset capable of participating in a much larger ecosystem of institutional capital, strategic liquidity opportunities, and long-term wealth creation. The goal is not simply to build a profitable business. The goal is to build a strategically valuable enterprise capable of generating transformational financial outcomes for decades to come.

The Founder Who Learned to Think Like Wall Street

Daniel Rivera started his business from a small apartment with an aging laptop, a folding table, and an idea that most people dismissed. At the time, he was thirty-two years old, working long hours as a freelance consultant while struggling to support his wife and two young children. Every month felt uncertain. Some months he earned enough to pay the bills comfortably, while other months forced him to juggle credit cards and negotiate payment extensions with vendors. Like many entrepreneurs, Daniel initially viewed business ownership as a way to escape employment and create more freedom for his family. He did not yet understand that businesses could become scalable financial assets capable of creating extraordinary wealth.

Daniel's first company focused on helping small businesses automate customer communication systems. Initially, he built every system himself, answered every client email personally, and handled every technical issue directly. Clients loved him because of his responsiveness and work ethic, but the business depended entirely on his constant labor. If Daniel stopped working, revenue stopped immediately. Although the company generated decent income, it lacked scalability.

One evening, Daniel attended a local entrepreneurship event where a private equity executive spoke about enterprise value. The executive explained that investors cared less about how hard founders worked and more about whether businesses could grow independently from the founders themselves. He described how scalable systems, recurring revenue, intellectual property, automation, and management infrastructure dramatically increased company valuations. Daniel listened carefully as the executive explained that some businesses sold for three times annual profit while others sold for twenty or thirty times earnings because investors believed in their scalability.

That night changed Daniel's thinking completely.

For the first time, he realized he had been building a job rather than a scalable asset. His business depended entirely on his personal involvement. There were no systems, no management layers, no automation, and no recurring subscription structure. Every new client required more hours of Daniel's time. Growth created stress rather than leverage.

Over the next two years, Daniel transformed the company systematically. He shifted from one-time consulting projects into subscription-based software services. He hired developers, customer support representatives, and operations managers. He documented workflows, automated onboarding systems, and created training programs so employees could handle most operational responsibilities independently. Revenue became recurring and predictable.

The transformation was difficult emotionally. Daniel struggled to let go of control. He worried employees would disappoint customers or damage the company's reputation. In the early stages, some mistakes happened exactly as he feared. However, he gradually realized that scalable businesses required systems rather than founder dependency. The more the company operated successfully without him, the more valuable it became.

By year five, the business had grown from a small consulting operation into a national SaaS platform serving thousands of clients across multiple industries. Revenue increased dramatically, but more importantly, investors began noticing the company. Venture capital firms reached out. Strategic acquirers requested meetings. Investment bankers introduced potential financing opportunities.

At first, Daniel became obsessed with the idea of selling the company immediately. The numbers seemed unbelievable compared to his previous life. One private equity firm offered a valuation nearly twenty times higher than anything he had ever imagined possible. But Daniel remembered another lesson from the private equity executive years earlier: optionality creates negotiating power. Instead of rushing into a sale, Daniel began studying advanced capital markets strategy seriously. He learned about IPOs, direct listings, secondary liquidity sales, debt financing, recapitalizations, and acquisition structures. He hired experienced advisors who helped him understand how institutional investors evaluated companies. Slowly, Daniel stopped thinking like a small business owner and started thinking like a capital allocator.

One of the smartest decisions Daniel made involved preserving strategic flexibility. Rather than accepting the first acquisition offer, he structured the company to support multiple future pathways. He improved financial reporting systems, strengthened governance structures, expanded the executive team, and diversified revenue streams. Investors began viewing the company as IPO-capable.

As the business continued growing, market conditions shifted favorably for technology companies. Valuation multiples expanded dramatically across the sector. Investment banks approached Daniel about taking the company public. Suddenly, the same business that once operated from a folding table in a small apartment was being discussed in terms of nine-figure valuations.

The IPO process was emotionally exhausting. Lawyers, accountants, underwriters, regulators, and institutional investors scrutinized every detail of the company. Daniel often felt overwhelmed by the pressure. However, he also recognized that the public markets offered opportunities far beyond a simple acquisition.

When the company finally went public, Daniel's life changed overnight—at least financially. On paper, his ownership stake became worth hundreds of millions of dollars. Media outlets featured his story as an example of entrepreneurial success. Investors praised the company's growth trajectory and scalable infrastructure.

But Daniel quickly learned another important lesson: liquidity and wealth are not always the same thing.

Most of his wealth remained tied to company stock. The share price fluctuated constantly based on earnings reports, market sentiment, interest rates, and broader economic conditions. Some weeks his net worth increased by tens of millions of dollars. Other weeks it declined sharply. Daniel realized that managing wealth after liquidity events required entirely different skills than building a business.

Fortunately, years of studying capital markets strategy had prepared him. Rather than making emotional decisions, Daniel developed a disciplined diversification plan. He sold portions of stock strategically over time, optimized taxes carefully, established trusts for his children, invested in real estate and private companies, and created a family office structure to manage long-term wealth.

Most importantly, Daniel avoided the mistake many founders make after major exits: losing purpose.

Instead of retiring completely, he used his public company equity strategically. He acquired smaller businesses, invested in emerging AI startups, and mentored younger entrepreneurs. His reputation in the capital markets ecosystem gave him access to opportunities he could never have imagined years earlier.

One day, during a private conference with young founders, Daniel shared the lesson that transformed his life.

“Most entrepreneurs think too small,” he explained. “They focus only on income. But real wealth comes from building scalable assets that institutional markets value highly. The goal isn’t just to work hard. The goal is to create systems, ownership, leverage, and optionality.”

A young founder in the audience asked him what the most important shift had been during his journey.

Daniel smiled. "The moment I stopped thinking like an employee inside my own business," he said, "and started thinking like Wall Street."

Chapter 2

Building Multiple Exit Paths and Maximizing Strategic Optionality

One of the greatest mistakes business owners make is building companies around only one possible future outcome. Many founders become emotionally attached to a single exit vision, such as selling the business to a large corporation, taking the company public, passing the business to family members, or maintaining ownership indefinitely. While there is nothing inherently wrong with any of these objectives, relying exclusively on one path creates vulnerability. Economic cycles shift, industries evolve, investor sentiment changes, technological disruption accelerates, and acquisition markets fluctuate constantly. Businesses that are structured around only one strategic outcome may struggle when market conditions move in an unfavorable direction. By contrast, companies that maintain multiple potential exit paths possess greater flexibility, stronger negotiating power, higher resilience, and often significantly greater long-term valuation potential.

Strategic optionality refers to the ability of a business to pursue multiple future liquidity events, financing structures, or ownership transitions depending on changing market conditions. Sophisticated founders intentionally build companies capable of adapting to different strategic opportunities rather than locking themselves into one predetermined destination. This flexibility becomes one of the most valuable assets a company can possess because investors, acquirers, and institutional capital providers place enormous value on businesses that can pivot intelligently as opportunities emerge.

The concept of multiple exit paths begins with understanding the various ways wealth can ultimately be created through business ownership. Some companies achieve liquidity through traditional acquisitions by strategic buyers. Others pursue mergers with private equity firms, direct listings, initial public offerings, management buyouts, recapitalizations, secondary share sales, or long-term dividend distribution strategies. Some founders even choose hybrid approaches that combine multiple liquidity events over time. A founder may initially sell a minority stake to private equity, later pursue an IPO, and eventually monetize additional equity through secondary sales while still retaining long-term ownership exposure.

One reason strategic optionality is so powerful is because market timing cannot always be predicted accurately. During certain economic cycles, acquisition markets become highly competitive, allowing founders to command premium valuations from strategic buyers. In other environments, IPO markets may offer stronger opportunities because public investors aggressively reward growth-oriented businesses. During periods of higher interest rates or economic uncertainty, private equity financing may become more restrictive, while strategic acquisitions by large corporations may increase as industry consolidation accelerates. Companies with flexible strategic positioning can shift toward whichever pathway offers the best valuation and long-term outcome at a given moment.

Founders who maintain multiple exit paths also gain tremendous leverage during negotiations. Businesses that desperately need a single outcome often negotiate from positions of weakness. For example, a company that must sell immediately due to liquidity pressure may accept lower valuations or unfavorable deal terms. By contrast, companies with strong cash flow, healthy balance sheets, scalable operations, and multiple strategic alternatives can negotiate aggressively because they are not dependent on any one transaction closing. Investors and acquirers recognize this leverage immediately, which often results in better pricing and more favorable deal structures.

Building strategic optionality requires intentional planning from the earliest stages of company development. One of the most important elements is maintaining strong financial discipline. Businesses with clean financial reporting, predictable revenue streams, transparent accounting systems, and healthy cash flow are far more adaptable to future strategic transactions. Whether pursuing acquisition opportunities, raising institutional capital, or preparing for public markets, sophisticated financial infrastructure dramatically expands future options.

Operational scalability also plays a major role in exit flexibility. Companies that rely heavily on founder involvement often become difficult to transition under acquisition or public market scenarios. Buyers and investors prefer businesses with professional management teams, documented systems, scalable infrastructure, and operational independence. Founders who intentionally build institutional-quality organizations increase the likelihood that multiple future pathways remain available simultaneously.

Corporate governance is another critical component of optionality. Businesses seeking institutional investment or public market access must demonstrate strong governance structures, compliance systems, legal organization, board oversight, and risk management processes. Many smaller businesses neglect these areas during early growth phases, only to discover later that weak governance limits financing opportunities or reduces acquisition interest. Strategic founders build governance systems early, even before they become immediately necessary, because they understand these structures create long-term flexibility.

Another essential factor in maximizing optionality involves industry positioning. Companies operating in fragmented industries often become attractive acquisition targets because larger corporations seek consolidation opportunities. Businesses operating in rapidly expanding sectors may attract venture capital or public market interest due to future growth expectations. Founders who understand how investors perceive their industries can position companies strategically to align with future capital demand.

Technology adoption has become increasingly important in preserving exit flexibility. Businesses that integrate automation, artificial intelligence, data analytics, subscription models, and scalable digital systems often maintain broader strategic opportunities than companies relying entirely on traditional manual operations. Institutional investors increasingly prioritize companies capable of generating scalable operating leverage through technology infrastructure.

Recurring revenue models are especially valuable when building multiple exit pathways. Subscription-based businesses, recurring service agreements, long-term contracts, membership platforms, and software-as-a-service models often command significantly higher valuations because they provide predictability and visibility into future cash flows. Predictable revenue allows acquirers and investors to forecast future performance more accurately, reducing perceived risk.

Brand positioning also influences optionality significantly. Strong brands create strategic value beyond immediate revenue generation. Businesses with trusted reputations, loyal customer communities, intellectual property assets, and recognizable market positioning may attract strategic buyers seeking market expansion opportunities. Public markets also tend to reward companies with compelling narratives and differentiated brand identities.

One of the most overlooked aspects of strategic optionality is personal founder flexibility. Some entrepreneurs unintentionally become emotionally trapped inside their businesses. Their personal identity becomes so closely connected to the company that rational strategic decision-making becomes difficult. Sophisticated founders maintain emotional discipline and evaluate opportunities objectively. They understand that preserving flexibility sometimes requires adjusting long-term plans as market realities evolve.

Many founders initially pursue rapid growth through aggressive venture capital financing without fully understanding how investor expectations may later influence exit options. Venture-backed companies often face pressure to pursue high-growth liquidity events such as IPOs or large acquisitions because institutional investors seek substantial returns within specific timelines. While venture capital can accelerate expansion dramatically, it may also reduce strategic flexibility if investor objectives diverge from founder goals. Advanced capital markets strategy therefore requires careful alignment between financing structures and long-term strategic vision.

Debt financing can sometimes preserve optionality more effectively than equity financing. While debt introduces repayment obligations and financial risk, it allows founders to access growth capital without immediately diluting ownership. Companies with strong cash flow may use debt strategically to fund acquisitions, expansion initiatives, or operational scaling while maintaining future flexibility around ownership and exit timing.

Private equity partnerships represent another increasingly important exit pathway. Many founders view private equity only as a final acquisition event, but sophisticated entrepreneurs often use private equity strategically in stages. Some founders sell minority stakes to private equity firms in order to access institutional expertise, operational resources, acquisition capital, and growth infrastructure while retaining majority ownership. Later, the company may pursue additional recapitalizations, public offerings, or strategic sales from a much stronger position.

Secondary liquidity markets have also expanded significantly in recent years. Founders no longer need to wait for full acquisitions or IPOs to create partial liquidity. Secondary share sales allow entrepreneurs to monetize portions of ownership while continuing to operate and grow their companies. This flexibility reduces personal financial pressure and often allows founders to make longer-term strategic decisions without being forced into premature exits.

International expansion can also enhance optionality dramatically. Companies with global growth potential often attract broader investor interest because international scalability increases total addressable market size. Strategic acquirers frequently pursue businesses capable of accelerating geographic expansion initiatives. Public markets similarly reward companies with large global growth narratives.

Another critical aspect of optionality involves intellectual property development. Proprietary technology, patents, data systems, algorithms, content libraries, brand assets, and unique operational methodologies can substantially increase strategic value. Intellectual property creates competitive barriers and increases acquisition interest because buyers often seek capabilities they cannot easily replicate internally.

Macroeconomic awareness becomes increasingly important as businesses grow larger. Interest rates, inflation, monetary policy, geopolitical events, and market sentiment all influence capital availability and valuation environments. Sophisticated founders monitor broader economic trends carefully because these factors shape financing conditions and liquidity opportunities. Companies with strategic flexibility can delay transactions during weak markets and accelerate activity during favorable conditions.

The psychological aspect of optionality should not be underestimated either. Businesses with multiple pathways generally operate from positions of confidence rather than desperation. Employees, investors, customers, and partners often recognize this stability, which can strengthen long-term relationships and reinforce organizational resilience. Strategic flexibility creates psychological leverage throughout the entire business ecosystem.

Many entrepreneurs assume that optionality only matters for massive corporations, but even smaller businesses benefit significantly from maintaining flexibility. A mid-sized business may choose between family succession planning, employee stock ownership plans, regional acquisitions, private equity recapitalizations, or strategic mergers depending on future conditions. The earlier founders understand these possibilities, the better they can structure businesses accordingly.

Long-term wealth creation often depends less on predicting one perfect outcome and more on preserving the ability to adapt intelligently as opportunities emerge. The business world changes rapidly, and rigid strategies frequently fail under evolving conditions. Companies that survive and thrive across decades are usually those capable of adjusting dynamically without losing operational stability or strategic direction.

The founders who create extraordinary wealth rarely depend entirely on luck or timing. Instead, they intentionally build businesses designed for adaptability, scalability, negotiation leverage, and strategic flexibility. They recognize that capital markets reward optionality because optionality reduces risk while increasing future opportunity potential.

As you continue building your own business or investment strategy, remember that every operational decision influences future flexibility. Ownership structures, financing choices, governance systems, technology infrastructure, branding, recurring revenue models, management development, and scalability planning all shape the range of future opportunities available to your company. The broader your strategic options become, the more powerful your long-term negotiating position may ultimately be.

The future belongs to businesses that can evolve intelligently as markets change. Strategic optionality is not simply a financial concept. It is a survival advantage, a valuation enhancer, and one of the most powerful wealth-building principles available to modern entrepreneurs.

The Company That Refused to Be Cornered

Sophia Bennett built her company during one of the most unstable economic periods in recent history. At thirty-six years old, she had already experienced both entrepreneurial success and painful business failure. Her first company, a boutique digital marketing agency, collapsed after losing two major clients during an economic downturn. The experience left her emotionally exhausted and financially damaged, but it also taught her one of the most important lessons of her life: dependence creates vulnerability.

Years later, Sophia launched a new company focused on AI-powered customer analytics software for retail businesses. From the beginning, she approached the business differently. She no longer wanted to build a company dependent on one client, one market condition, one investor, or one future exit path. She wanted flexibility.

The early years were difficult. Investors repeatedly encouraged Sophia to pursue aggressive venture capital financing in exchange for rapid expansion. Several advisors told her she needed to "grow at all costs" if she wanted to compete against larger technology firms. But Sophia remembered the helplessness she had felt during her first business collapse. She refused to build a company that could be cornered by changing market conditions.

Instead of relying entirely on venture capital, Sophia built the company gradually using a combination of recurring subscription revenue, disciplined operational spending, strategic debt financing, and selective institutional partnerships. Growth happened more slowly initially, but the company remained financially stable and highly adaptable.

Sophia also made another unusual decision early in the company's development. Rather than focusing exclusively on one future exit strategy, she intentionally structured the business to support multiple possible outcomes. She hired experienced financial professionals, implemented institutional accounting systems, built a strong management team, and invested heavily in scalable operational infrastructure. Some employees questioned why she spent so much money preparing systems "far ahead of schedule."

Sophia understood something they did not.

She wasn't preparing for one future. She was preparing for many possible futures.

As the company grew, larger competitors began paying attention. A publicly traded software corporation approached Sophia with an acquisition proposal that would have made her personally wealthy overnight. Many people urged her to accept immediately. The valuation seemed enormous compared to where she had started.

But Sophia hesitated.

The company's revenue was growing rapidly. Customer retention remained exceptionally strong. International demand had started emerging organically. More importantly, Sophia recognized that the business still possessed enormous untapped potential.

Rather than rejecting the acquisition outright, she used the offer strategically.

Because the company had strong financial systems and multiple financing alternatives available, Sophia did not negotiate from desperation. She understood that her company could remain private successfully, pursue institutional growth financing, or potentially enter public markets in the future. That optionality dramatically strengthened her negotiating position.

Over the next eighteen months, Sophia continued expanding carefully. She launched international operations, introduced AI automation features, and completed several strategic acquisitions using a combination of cash flow and financing partnerships. Revenue accelerated even faster than expected.

Then the economy changed.

Interest rates rose sharply. Venture capital markets tightened. Many high-growth technology companies began collapsing under unsustainable operating losses. Businesses that had depended entirely on continuous investor funding suddenly faced severe liquidity crises.

Sophia's company remained stable.

Because she had prioritized recurring revenue, operational discipline, and financial flexibility, the company generated healthy cash flow even during difficult market conditions. Competitors began laying off employees aggressively while Sophia's business continued expanding internationally.

Soon, a private equity consortium approached her with a completely different proposal.

Rather than acquiring the entire business outright, the consortium offered to purchase a minority stake while helping finance additional acquisitions and long-term expansion. Sophia would retain operational control while gaining access to institutional capital and strategic resources.

Again, Sophia evaluated the opportunity carefully.

Many founders become emotionally reactive during negotiations, but Sophia approached decisions strategically. She analyzed valuation implications, dilution effects, governance structures, liquidity opportunities, tax consequences, and long-term optionality. After months of negotiations, she agreed to a carefully structured partnership that allowed her to take partial liquidity while still maintaining majority ownership.

The transaction transformed her personal financial life.

For the first time, Sophia achieved significant liquidity without giving up control of the company she had spent years building. She paid off debt, diversified investments, purchased real estate, and established long-term financial security for her family. But perhaps most importantly, the liquidity reduced emotional pressure. Now she could think even longer term. Over the next several years, the company expanded globally. The private equity partnership accelerated acquisitions, strengthened infrastructure, and positioned the company for future public market opportunities. Investment banks began discussing IPO scenarios regularly.

Sophia noticed something fascinating during this period.

The more optionality the company possessed, the more valuable it became.

Institutional investors loved the company because it could remain private profitably, pursue a strategic acquisition, or enter public markets successfully depending on future conditions. That flexibility reduced perceived risk while increasing future opportunity potential.

Eventually, after careful market analysis, Sophia and her advisors concluded that public markets offered the strongest long-term opportunity. Investor demand for AI-driven enterprise software companies had surged again, and the company's international expansion story attracted significant institutional interest.

The IPO became one of the most successful public offerings of the year.

Financial media celebrated Sophia as a visionary founder who had navigated multiple economic cycles successfully while preserving ownership and operational control. But privately, Sophia understood the deeper reason behind the company's success.

She had never allowed the business to become trapped by one future outcome.

Years later, during an interview at a global entrepreneurship conference, a young founder asked Sophia what separated resilient companies from fragile ones.

Sophia paused before answering.

"Most businesses fail because they build themselves into corners," she explained. "They depend on one investor, one customer, one market condition, or one exit strategy. But markets always change. Capital flows change. Industries change."

The founder asked her what entrepreneurs should focus on instead.

Sophia smiled.

"Build flexibility," she said. "Build systems strong enough that you always have options. The more strategic choices you preserve, the more powerful your company becomes."

The audience applauded politely, but Sophia knew most people still underestimated the importance of optionality.

They would eventually learn the lesson the same way she had—through experience.

Chapter 3

Increasing Company Valuation Through Scalability, Positioning, and Investor Psychology

One of the most misunderstood concepts in entrepreneurship is business valuation. Many business owners believe valuation is determined simply by revenue, annual profit, or the number of years a company has been operating. While financial performance certainly matters, sophisticated investors evaluate businesses through a far more complex lens. Two companies generating identical profits may receive dramatically different valuations depending on scalability, industry positioning, growth potential, operational structure, investor perception, recurring revenue quality, and long-term strategic opportunity. Understanding how valuation truly works is one of the most powerful skills an entrepreneur can develop because even small improvements in valuation multiples can create enormous increases in long-term wealth.

At its core, valuation reflects perceived future opportunity. Investors are not simply buying current revenue or present earnings; they are purchasing expectations about the future. A business with modest current profits but extraordinary scalability may command far higher valuations than a business generating large cash flow with limited growth potential. This principle explains why many technology companies, subscription platforms, AI businesses, and scalable digital enterprises achieve valuations that appear disconnected from present earnings. Investors believe future expansion potential justifies premium pricing.

Scalability is one of the primary drivers of modern business valuation. Scalable businesses possess the ability to increase revenue substantially without proportional increases in operating costs. In other words, the business can grow efficiently while maintaining or improving profit margins. Companies that require significant increases in labor, infrastructure, or operational complexity for every additional dollar of revenue generally receive lower valuation multiples because growth becomes more difficult to sustain over time.

Software-as-a-service companies provide one of the clearest examples of scalability. Once the software infrastructure has been developed, the company can often add thousands of additional users with relatively small incremental costs. This creates expanding margins as revenue grows. Investors reward this type of operating leverage because it allows businesses to compound profitability rapidly over time. By contrast, businesses heavily dependent on manual labor or founder involvement may struggle to achieve similar scalability.

This does not mean traditional businesses cannot achieve high valuations. Many service businesses, manufacturing companies, healthcare organizations, education businesses, financial firms, and real estate enterprises have created enormous wealth. However, the highest-valued companies within these industries usually find ways to systemize operations, automate processes, create recurring revenue streams, strengthen brand positioning, and reduce dependence on founder labor. The more scalable the underlying business model becomes, the more attractive the company appears to institutional investors.

Recurring revenue is another major driver of valuation expansion. Predictable cash flow reduces uncertainty for investors and allows more accurate forecasting of future performance. Subscription businesses, maintenance contracts, licensing agreements, membership programs, SaaS platforms, insurance renewals, financial advisory relationships, and recurring service models often receive higher valuation multiples than businesses relying entirely on one-time transactions. Predictability creates confidence, and confidence increases valuation. Customer retention metrics also influence valuation significantly. Businesses that retain customers for long periods often possess stronger economic durability than companies forced to replace customers constantly. High retention rates reduce customer acquisition costs over time and increase lifetime customer value. Investors study retention patterns carefully because recurring customer behavior often indicates strong product-market fit, operational consistency, and long-term sustainability.

Another major factor affecting valuation is total addressable market size. Investors prefer businesses operating within industries capable of supporting significant future growth. A company dominating a tiny niche market may eventually face growth limitations, while a company positioned within a rapidly expanding global market may continue scaling for years or decades. This is why founders spend substantial time communicating market opportunity size during fundraising presentations, acquisition negotiations, and IPO roadshows.

Industry trends also shape investor psychology dramatically. Markets tend to reward businesses aligned with major technological, demographic, economic, or cultural shifts. Artificial intelligence, automation, renewable energy, cybersecurity, digital education, fintech, health technology, creator economies, and data analytics have all experienced periods of strong investor enthusiasm because markets perceive large future growth opportunities within these sectors. Companies positioned within favorable long-term trends often command premium valuations even before maximizing profitability.

Brand positioning creates another layer of strategic value. Strong brands build trust, emotional connection, customer loyalty, and market differentiation. Investors recognize that trusted brands often possess pricing power, customer retention advantages, and long-term competitive resilience. Brand equity can become an intangible asset worth billions of dollars over time. Some companies are acquired less for current profits and more for the strength of their customer relationships, audience loyalty, and market influence.

Intellectual property further strengthens valuation potential. Patents, proprietary technology, algorithms, trademarks, content libraries, customer data systems, operational methodologies, and unique product innovations create defensibility within competitive markets. Investors prefer businesses with barriers to entry because defensibility protects long-term profitability. Companies without differentiation often face pricing pressure and competitive erosion over time.

Management quality also plays a major role in valuation psychology. Institutional investors frequently state that they invest in people as much as products. Strong leadership teams inspire confidence because investors believe experienced operators can navigate uncertainty effectively. Companies with weak leadership structures or excessive founder dependency may receive discounted valuations because operational continuity becomes uncertain.

This is one reason professional management infrastructure becomes increasingly important as businesses scale. Founders who build capable executive teams, operational systems, financial controls, and governance structures often increase enterprise value significantly. Investors prefer companies that can continue functioning effectively even if the founder becomes less involved operationally.

Financial reporting quality represents another major valuation factor. Businesses with transparent accounting systems, audited financial statements, predictable reporting procedures, and institutional-grade financial controls are generally viewed as lower risk. Weak reporting systems create uncertainty, and uncertainty reduces investor confidence. Sophisticated entrepreneurs therefore invest heavily in financial infrastructure long before liquidity events occur.

Growth rate is obviously important as well, but growth quality matters just as much as growth speed. Investors increasingly distinguish between sustainable growth and artificially inflated expansion. Businesses generating growth through unsustainable spending, poor customer economics, or excessive leverage may face valuation compression later. Companies with efficient customer acquisition models, strong margins, healthy retention, and disciplined expansion often receive stronger long-term investor support.

Profit margins influence valuation differently depending on industry and business stage. Early-stage growth companies may intentionally prioritize expansion over profitability, while mature companies are generally expected to demonstrate strong operational efficiency. Investors evaluate margin structures carefully because margins reveal the underlying economics of the business model. Companies capable of expanding margins over time often achieve premium valuations.

Capital efficiency has also become increasingly important in modern markets. Investors now pay closer attention to how effectively companies deploy capital. Businesses capable of generating substantial growth without excessive financing requirements often appear more attractive because they preserve flexibility and reduce dilution risk. Founders who understand capital allocation strategy can increase valuation by demonstrating disciplined financial management. Macroeconomic conditions strongly influence valuation environments as well. Interest rates, inflation, liquidity conditions, monetary policy, and investor sentiment all affect how aggressively markets price growth opportunities. During low interest rate environments, investors often pay higher multiples for future earnings because capital becomes abundant and borrowing costs decline. During tighter monetary periods, valuation multiples frequently compress as investors prioritize stability and profitability.

Public market comparables also affect private company valuations. Investment bankers, venture capital firms, and institutional investors constantly analyze publicly traded peers to estimate valuation ranges for private businesses. If comparable public companies experience strong market performance, private valuations within the same sector often rise as well. This relationship demonstrates how broader market psychology influences company value.

Storytelling and narrative positioning play surprisingly large roles in valuation expansion. Markets are emotional systems influenced by optimism, fear, momentum, and perception. Founders capable of communicating compelling visions often attract stronger investor enthusiasm. This does not mean exaggeration or manipulation. Instead, it means articulating how the business fits within larger economic or technological trends and why future growth opportunities are substantial. The best founders learn how to combine strong operational execution with strategic narrative positioning. They understand that numbers alone rarely maximize valuation. Investors must also believe in the long-term story behind the company. This is why IPO roadshows, investor presentations, branding campaigns, and public relations strategies become so important during major capital events.

Another important valuation principle involves scarcity. Rare businesses often command premium pricing because investors compete aggressively for limited opportunities. Companies with unique technology, dominant market positioning, exceptional growth metrics, or highly scalable infrastructure may generate bidding competition among investors or acquirers. Competition itself often drives valuations substantially higher.

Timing also matters enormously. Some businesses pursue liquidity events during periods of peak investor enthusiasm, while others enter markets during unfavorable cycles. Sophisticated founders monitor industry momentum, capital flows, and market sentiment carefully because valuation environments fluctuate continuously. A company may receive dramatically different valuations depending on macroeconomic timing alone.

Emotional discipline becomes critical throughout this process. Many founders either overestimate or underestimate company value due to emotional attachment. Advanced capital markets strategy requires objective analysis rather than ego-driven decision-making. Sophisticated entrepreneurs focus on building genuine enterprise quality rather than chasing superficial valuation metrics.

Long-term wealth creation ultimately depends on understanding that valuation is not static. Valuation can be engineered strategically over time through scalability improvements, recurring revenue expansion, operational optimization, brand development, intellectual property creation, management strengthening, and market positioning. Founders who intentionally build businesses around these principles often create exponentially greater financial outcomes than those who focus only on short-term profitability.

As businesses evolve, founders must begin thinking like institutional investors themselves. They must ask how investors perceive risk, growth potential, scalability, defensibility, and future opportunity. The entrepreneurs who create extraordinary wealth are usually those who understand how markets value businesses psychologically as well as financially.

In the modern economy, valuation represents far more than a number attached to a company. It reflects investor confidence, future expectations, strategic positioning, operational scalability, and market perception simultaneously. Entrepreneurs who understand these dynamics gain the ability to shape how markets view their businesses, which ultimately influences access to capital, acquisition opportunities, liquidity events, and long-term wealth creation potential.

The future belongs to businesses capable of scaling efficiently, communicating compelling visions, and aligning themselves with long-term market demand. Founders who master valuation psychology position themselves not only to build profitable companies but also to create transformational enterprise value capable of generating generational wealth.

The Valuation Gap

When Marcus Delgado started his logistics company, nobody considered it extraordinary. The business focused on helping small regional retailers manage shipping coordination and warehouse efficiency. The company generated steady revenue, but growth was slow, margins were average, and operations depended heavily on Marcus personally solving problems every day.

For years, Marcus viewed success through a simple lens: annual income. If the company earned enough profit to support his family comfortably, he considered the business successful. He paid himself aggressively, purchased luxury vehicles as revenue increased, and treated the company primarily as a source of lifestyle income rather than a scalable asset.

Then something unexpected happened.

One of Marcus's longtime friends, Ethan, sold a software company for nearly twenty times annual revenue. Marcus was shocked because Ethan's company generated less annual profit than his logistics business. Confused, Marcus asked how such a valuation was even possible.

Ethan explained one word.

"Scalability."

At first, Marcus dismissed the idea as another Silicon Valley buzzword. But curiosity pushed him to study deeper. The more he learned about capital markets, the more uncomfortable he became. He realized investors did not value businesses based only on current income. They valued future opportunity, recurring revenue, operational leverage, scalability, and growth potential.

Marcus suddenly saw his own business differently.

The company depended entirely on him. Every operational problem reached his desk. Revenue came mostly from customized service contracts that required heavy manual involvement. There was little automation, no proprietary technology, limited recurring subscription income, and almost no operational infrastructure independent from Marcus personally.

The business produced income.

But it lacked enterprise value.

That realization changed everything.

Over the next several years, Marcus transformed the company methodically. Instead of operating purely as a traditional logistics coordinator, he invested heavily in software development and data systems. He built a proprietary logistics optimization platform that automated inventory forecasting, shipping route analysis, and warehouse efficiency recommendations for retailers.

The transition was expensive and emotionally difficult.

Many employees resisted the changes. Some longtime clients disliked moving toward standardized systems rather than custom manual service. Revenue growth slowed temporarily while Marcus reinvested aggressively into technology infrastructure and operational systems.

Friends questioned his decisions constantly.

"You already make good money," one friend told him. "Why take all this risk?"

Marcus struggled with the same question privately. But he had begun thinking differently about business ownership. He no longer wanted only income. He wanted scalability.

The software platform eventually transformed the economics of the company completely.

Instead of relying entirely on labor-intensive consulting contracts, the business began generating recurring subscription revenue. Margins expanded dramatically because software clients could be added without proportional increases in labor costs. Customer retention improved because clients integrated the platform deeply into their operations.

Most importantly, the company no longer depended entirely on Marcus personally.

He hired executives, created management systems, documented operational procedures, and implemented institutional financial reporting. Gradually, the business evolved from a founder-dependent operation into a scalable technology-enabled platform.

Investors began noticing. A venture capital firm approached Marcus first, offering growth financing at a valuation nearly five times higher than anything he had previously imagined possible. Marcus declined initially, choosing instead to continue strengthening the business independently.

Then larger opportunities appeared.

Private equity groups requested meetings. Strategic acquirers reached out. Investment banks introduced potential expansion financing structures. Industry analysts began mentioning the company as an emerging player within logistics automation technology.

Marcus became fascinated by how differently markets viewed his company now compared to earlier years.

The core industry had not changed dramatically. The company still operated within logistics and supply chain management. But because the business model had become scalable, recurring, technology-driven, and systemized, valuation perceptions shifted completely.

One evening, Marcus reviewed financial reports with his CFO, Elena.

"We actually make less net income today than we did three years ago," Marcus observed. "But investors think we're worth ten times more." Elena smiled. "Because they're valuing the future," she explained.

That sentence stayed with Marcus permanently.

As the company continued scaling nationally, public market conditions became increasingly favorable for AI-driven logistics technology companies. Comparable public businesses traded at enormous valuation multiples due to investor enthusiasm surrounding automation and supply chain optimization.

Investment bankers suggested the company could potentially pursue an IPO within two years.

The idea terrified Marcus initially.

Years earlier, he had simply wanted stable income. Now Wall Street institutions discussed nine-figure and potentially ten-figure valuation scenarios.

Marcus began studying investor psychology obsessively. He realized valuation was influenced not only by numbers but also by narrative positioning, market sentiment, scalability expectations, and competitive differentiation. He worked closely with advisors to refine the company's positioning carefully.

The company was no longer presented as a traditional logistics provider. It became positioned as an AI-powered infrastructure platform helping modern retailers optimize global supply chain efficiency through predictive automation systems.

The underlying business had evolved—but so had the story surrounding it.

When the IPO eventually launched, investor demand exceeded expectations dramatically. The company's valuation surged far beyond initial projections. Financial media praised Marcus as an innovative entrepreneur transforming traditional logistics through technology.

But privately, Marcus knew the truth.

The biggest transformation had not occurred inside the company.

It had occurred inside his own thinking.

Years earlier, he viewed business purely as a way to generate income. Now he understood that scalable enterprise value represented an entirely different category of wealth creation.

Months after the IPO, Marcus spoke at an entrepreneurship conference attended by hundreds of small business owners.

During the question-and-answer session, one entrepreneur asked him what lesson had changed his life most significantly.

Marcus paused thoughtfully before responding. "Most founders work incredibly hard," he said. "But hard work alone doesn't create massive valuations. Markets reward scalability, predictability, systems, and future opportunity."

The entrepreneur asked him how business owners should start thinking differently.

Marcus smiled.

"Ask yourself one question every day," he said. "If you disappeared tomorrow, would your company still grow?"

The room became quiet.

Because everyone immediately understood the deeper meaning behind the question.

That question separated ordinary businesses from scalable assets.

And scalable assets were what created extraordinary wealth.

Chapter 4

Institutional Investors, Private Equity, and the Mechanics of Large-Scale Capital

One of the defining differences between small businesses and highly valuable enterprises is access to institutional capital. Many entrepreneurs spend years focusing almost exclusively on customers, operations, and revenue generation without fully understanding how institutional investors influence business growth, valuation, and long-term wealth creation. Yet some of the largest companies in the world reached their scale because they learned how to attract and deploy outside capital strategically. Institutional investors—including private equity firms, venture capital funds, hedge funds, pension funds, sovereign wealth funds, family offices, and investment banks—play a central role in the modern capital markets ecosystem. Business owners who understand how these institutions think gain a tremendous strategic advantage because they begin building companies in ways that align with institutional demand.

Institutional capital operates differently from personal investing. While individual investors may sometimes make emotional decisions or invest based on intuition alone, institutional investors usually follow highly structured frameworks designed to evaluate scalability, risk, return potential, management quality, market positioning, operational efficiency, and long-term growth opportunities. These institutions manage enormous amounts of capital and seek opportunities capable of generating significant returns while balancing risk exposure. Entrepreneurs who understand these priorities can position their businesses much more effectively for financing, partnerships, acquisitions, and future liquidity events.

Private equity has become one of the most influential forces in global business over the past several decades. Private equity firms raise large pools of capital from institutional investors and deploy that capital into businesses they believe possess strong growth or operational improvement potential. Unlike traditional stock market investing, private equity firms often take active ownership roles within the businesses they acquire or finance. They may restructure operations, improve management systems, pursue acquisitions, optimize capital allocation, expand internationally, or prepare companies for future exits such as IPOs or strategic sales.

Many entrepreneurs misunderstand private equity because they assume these firms are only interested in buying struggling businesses or taking control away from founders. While some private equity strategies involve distressed turnarounds, many firms specifically seek healthy businesses with scalable foundations and capable management teams. In many cases, private equity firms become strategic growth partners rather than adversaries. They may provide operational expertise, acquisition resources, industry relationships, financial discipline, and institutional infrastructure that accelerate growth dramatically.

Understanding how private equity evaluates businesses can help founders increase company value substantially. Private equity investors typically focus on predictable cash flow, operational scalability, recurring revenue, margin expansion potential, defensible market positioning, and opportunities for future valuation growth. They often look for businesses capable of generating consistent earnings while still possessing meaningful expansion opportunities. Businesses that combine operational stability with future scalability frequently attract the strongest institutional interest.

One important concept in private equity is leverage. Many private equity transactions involve the use of debt financing alongside investor capital. This structure, commonly known as a leveraged buyout, allows firms to amplify returns by using borrowed capital strategically. If the acquired company grows successfully and increases profitability, equity investors may generate substantial returns relative to the original equity investment. However, leverage also introduces financial risk, especially during economic downturns or operational disruptions.

Founders considering private equity partnerships must therefore understand both the opportunities and responsibilities associated with leveraged growth structures. While leverage can accelerate expansion and increase investor returns, excessive debt can create operational pressure and reduce flexibility during difficult market conditions. Sophisticated entrepreneurs learn how to balance growth ambition with financial resilience.

Venture capital represents another important segment of institutional investing, particularly for high-growth startups and technology-driven companies. Venture capital firms generally invest earlier in the corporate lifecycle than traditional private equity firms. These investors often prioritize scalability, market disruption potential, innovation, and future growth rather than current profitability. Many venture-backed businesses intentionally operate at losses during early growth stages because investors prioritize rapid market expansion and future dominance over immediate earnings. The venture capital ecosystem has helped finance some of the largest companies in modern history, including businesses within technology, artificial intelligence, fintech, biotech, social media, and software infrastructure. However, venture capital also introduces unique pressures. Venture investors often seek extremely large returns because many early-stage investments fail completely. As a result, founders may face aggressive growth expectations, dilution, governance oversight, and pressure to pursue large liquidity events within defined timelines.

Not every business should pursue venture capital. Many businesses grow more effectively through disciplined organic expansion, strategic debt financing, or selective institutional partnerships rather than hypergrowth models. Entrepreneurs must align financing strategies with the nature of their industries, operational goals, personal risk tolerance, and long-term vision. The wrong type of capital can create unnecessary pressure and strategic misalignment.

Family offices have also become increasingly important within the institutional capital ecosystem. Family offices manage wealth for ultra-high-net-worth individuals or multigenerational wealthy families. Unlike some institutional investors focused heavily on short-term performance metrics, family offices often pursue longer investment horizons and flexible partnership structures. Many founders prefer working with family offices because these investors may prioritize relationship quality, strategic alignment, and sustainable growth over rapid exit timelines.

Sovereign wealth funds, pension funds, and insurance companies also participate heavily in global capital markets. These institutions often allocate capital into private equity funds, infrastructure investments, real estate portfolios, technology platforms, and public equities in order to generate long-term returns. Although entrepreneurs may not interact directly with these institutions initially, their capital frequently flows through investment funds that eventually finance growing businesses.

Institutional investors place enormous emphasis on management quality. One of the most common phrases within private equity and venture capital is that investors "bet on people." Strong leadership teams inspire confidence because investors know market conditions, technologies, and industries can change rapidly. Businesses led by adaptable, disciplined, and strategically intelligent management teams often receive stronger institutional support even during periods of uncertainty.

This is why founders must eventually transition from being pure operators into organizational leaders. Small businesses often revolve around founder execution, but institutional-scale companies require delegation, executive leadership development, governance structures, and operational systems capable of supporting large-scale growth. Founders who refuse to evolve operationally may limit institutional interest because investors worry about scalability and continuity risks.

Financial reporting and transparency also become critically important as businesses seek institutional partnerships. Institutional investors require accurate reporting, forecasting systems, compliance infrastructure, legal organization, and operational visibility. Many smaller businesses lack these systems initially, which can significantly reduce valuation or delay financing opportunities. Sophisticated entrepreneurs build institutional-quality infrastructure long before major transactions occur because preparation itself increases flexibility and credibility.

Another important factor institutional investors evaluate is market defensibility. Businesses operating in highly competitive environments without differentiation may struggle to maintain long-term profitability. Investors therefore seek companies possessing barriers to entry such as proprietary technology, strong brands, intellectual property, customer loyalty, regulatory advantages, network effects, or unique operational efficiencies. Defensibility protects long-term margins and reduces competitive risk.

Institutional capital also flows heavily toward industries perceived as having strong secular growth trends. Artificial intelligence, automation, renewable energy, cybersecurity, digital health, cloud computing, fintech, education technology, creator economies, and advanced data infrastructure have all attracted enormous institutional investment because investors believe these sectors possess long-term expansion potential. Businesses aligned with powerful market trends often gain access to capital more easily because investors anticipate future demand growth.

One of the most important lessons entrepreneurs must understand is that institutional investors evaluate risk differently than founders do. Founders often become emotionally attached to products, ideas, or operational details. Institutional investors focus more objectively on scalability, return potential, downside protection, competitive positioning, and financial outcomes. Learning how investors think allows entrepreneurs to communicate more effectively and structure businesses strategically.

Board governance becomes increasingly important as institutional capital enters a business. Investors frequently seek board representation or governance oversight rights in order to monitor company performance and influence strategic decisions. Strong boards can add tremendous value through experience, industry connections, financial discipline, and strategic guidance. However, governance complexity also increases as companies scale institutionally.

Another major concept within institutional investing is exit planning. Institutional investors generally require eventual liquidity pathways in order to realize returns. These exits may occur through IPOs, acquisitions, recapitalizations, secondary sales, or mergers. Entrepreneurs must therefore think carefully about how future liquidity events align with personal goals and operational strategy.

The relationship between institutional investors and founders can become extraordinarily powerful when aligned properly. Many of the world's largest companies achieved massive scale through collaborative partnerships between visionary founders and disciplined institutional capital providers. When founders combine innovation, operational execution, and strategic vision with institutional financial resources and expertise, extraordinary wealth creation can occur.

However, founders must also maintain strategic awareness throughout the process. Not all capital is equal. Some investors create value through expertise and long-term alignment, while others may prioritize short-term financial engineering or aggressive control structures. Sophisticated entrepreneurs evaluate investors as carefully as investors evaluate companies.

Negotiation skill becomes increasingly important as institutional relationships develop. Deal structures involving valuation, dilution, governance rights, liquidation preferences, debt covenants, equity incentives, and operational control can dramatically influence long-term founder outcomes. Entrepreneurs who fail to understand these mechanics may unintentionally sacrifice enormous future wealth or control.

One of the most valuable aspects of institutional capital is the acceleration effect it can create. Businesses that might take decades to scale organically can sometimes achieve rapid expansion through strategic financing, acquisitions, technology investment, and global infrastructure development. Capital acts as fuel, but only when combined with strong operational execution and strategic discipline.

Institutional investors also value optionality. Companies capable of pursuing multiple future liquidity pathways often command stronger valuations because flexibility reduces risk and expands opportunity potential. Businesses prepared for acquisitions, IPOs, strategic partnerships, or long-term private ownership maintain stronger negotiating positions throughout capital discussions.

Ultimately, understanding institutional capital is about learning how large-scale wealth creation actually functions within the modern economy. The world's most successful companies rarely scale through operational execution alone. They scale through intelligent combinations of capital, leadership, systems, market positioning, investor confidence, and strategic timing.

Entrepreneurs who understand these systems gain the ability to move beyond small business thinking into enterprise-building strategy. They begin viewing capital not simply as money but as a strategic resource capable of accelerating growth, expanding optionality, increasing valuation, and creating transformational long-term wealth.

The modern economy rewards founders who understand both entrepreneurship and capital allocation. Businesses capable of attracting institutional confidence often gain access to opportunities unavailable to ordinary companies. The ability to navigate these relationships intelligently can fundamentally alter the trajectory of both a business and the personal wealth of its founders.

The Investor Meeting That Changed Everything

When Olivia Carter started her healthcare technology company, she had no intention of raising institutional capital. She had watched other founders lose control of their businesses after accepting outside investors, and she promised herself she would never allow that to happen.

Her company developed software that helped independent medical clinics automate insurance verification, patient scheduling, and billing workflows. The idea came from years of frustration while helping manage her father's small medical office. She believed the healthcare system wasted enormous amounts of time and money due to inefficient administrative processes.

Initially, Olivia bootstrapped the company using personal savings and modest business revenue. She hired a small development team, rented a tiny office, and worked constantly. The business grew steadily because clinics desperately needed efficiency improvements. Within four years, the company generated millions in recurring annual revenue while remaining profitable.

Friends constantly encouraged Olivia to pursue venture capital financing. "You're growing too slowly," one advisor warned her repeatedly. "Competitors are raising huge amounts of money."

But Olivia resisted. She feared losing independence more than she desired rapid expansion.

Then market conditions shifted unexpectedly.

Large hospital systems began aggressively investing in healthcare automation technology. Venture-backed competitors expanded quickly, hiring massive sales teams and launching national marketing campaigns. Some competitors operated at heavy losses while using investor capital to dominate market share aggressively.

For the first time, Olivia felt pressure.

Her company remained profitable and stable, but competitors began growing faster due to institutional financing advantages. Recruiters poached employees aggressively using stock incentives and higher salaries funded by investor capital. Industry conferences increasingly focused on highly funded startups rather than smaller independent companies.

One evening, Olivia reviewed growth projections with her CFO, Daniel.

"If we continue expanding organically," Daniel explained, "we'll probably remain profitable and successful. But we may eventually lose the opportunity to become a dominant national platform."

Olivia understood the implication immediately.

Without capital, growth would remain limited.

Still, she hesitated.

A few weeks later, an old mentor introduced Olivia to a healthcare-focused private equity firm known for partnering collaboratively with founders rather than replacing them. Reluctantly, she agreed to an introductory meeting.

That meeting changed everything.

Instead of pressuring Olivia aggressively, the investors spent hours asking thoughtful questions about operational systems, customer retention, product scalability, and long-term industry trends. They clearly understood healthcare infrastructure deeply. More importantly, they respected the company's disciplined financial management and profitability.

For the first time, Olivia realized institutional capital was not always about taking control away from founders.

Sometimes it was about acceleration.

Over the next several months, Olivia studied institutional investing obsessively. She learned how private equity firms evaluated businesses, how leverage worked, how governance structures operated, and how scaling infrastructure influenced valuation. The more she learned, the more her perspective evolved.

She realized her fear had come from misunderstanding capital itself.

Capital was neither good nor bad.

It was simply a tool.

Used recklessly, it could destroy businesses. Used intelligently, it could multiply opportunity dramatically.

Eventually, Olivia negotiated a minority investment partnership with the private equity firm. The structure allowed her to retain majority ownership and operational control while gaining access to substantial growth capital, acquisition resources, executive recruiting support, and institutional infrastructure.

The transformation happened rapidly.

The company expanded into new states, hired experienced executives, improved cybersecurity infrastructure, and acquired two smaller competitors. Revenue accelerated dramatically while operational systems became more sophisticated and scalable.

Olivia also noticed something surprising about herself.

She had changed as a leader.

Before institutional involvement, she focused mostly on operations and survival. Now she thought strategically about scalability, market positioning, acquisitions, valuation expansion, and long-term capital markets opportunities.

The investors challenged her constantly.

They asked difficult questions about margins, growth efficiency, defensibility, pricing strategy, and future liquidity pathways. Initially, Olivia found these conversations stressful. But over time, she realized the pressure was making both her and the company stronger.

Several years later, the business had become one of the fastest-growing healthcare automation platforms in the country. Public market analysts began discussing the company as a potential IPO candidate.

One afternoon, Olivia sat in a conference room overlooking Manhattan while investment bankers presented public market valuation projections.

The numbers stunned her.

The company's estimated valuation exceeded anything she had once believed possible.

As the bankers discussed investor appetite and market timing, Olivia thought back to her earlier fear of institutional capital. She smiled quietly to herself.

The real danger had never been capital.

The real danger would have been refusing to learn how the system worked.

Months later, during a panel discussion for female entrepreneurs, an audience member asked Olivia whether founders should avoid outside investors.

Olivia paused carefully before answering.

"Bad partnerships are dangerous," she said honestly. "But smart capital, aligned correctly, can change the trajectory of your company forever."

The audience listened closely.

Olivia continued.

"The key is understanding that institutional investors aren't just funding businesses. They're evaluating scalability, leadership, systems, positioning, and long-term opportunity. Once you understand how they think, you stop fearing capital markets."

Another entrepreneur asked what lesson mattered most.

Olivia smiled.

"Learn the language of capital before you need capital," she said. "Because the founders who understand institutional money gain access to opportunities most businesses never even see."

Chapter 5

Timing the Market, Economic Cycles, and the Psychology of Capital Flows

One of the most important yet least predictable aspects of advanced capital markets strategy is timing. Businesses do not operate in isolation. Every company exists within a broader economic environment shaped by interest rates, investor sentiment, inflation, liquidity conditions, geopolitical events, technological shifts, regulatory changes, and macroeconomic cycles. These forces influence how capital moves throughout the economy and dramatically affect business valuations, financing availability, acquisition activity, and liquidity opportunities. Founders who understand economic cycles and investor psychology gain a major advantage because they can position their companies strategically before conditions change rather than reacting after opportunities disappear.

Many entrepreneurs focus almost exclusively on internal business operations while underestimating how external market conditions shape long-term outcomes. A company may execute brilliantly operationally yet still struggle to raise capital during periods of economic contraction. Conversely, even moderately successful businesses may achieve extraordinary valuations during periods of strong investor optimism and abundant liquidity. This reality does not mean founders should attempt to predict markets perfectly. Instead, it means sophisticated entrepreneurs must develop awareness of how capital behaves during different economic environments.

Capital flows through markets in cycles. During expansionary periods, investors generally become more optimistic and willing to take risk. Interest rates often remain lower, financing becomes easier to obtain, valuation multiples expand, and liquidity events such as IPOs and acquisitions increase dramatically. Investors search aggressively for growth opportunities because abundant capital seeks strong returns. During these periods, businesses capable of demonstrating scalability, innovation, and market momentum may achieve extremely favorable financing conditions and premium valuations.

During contractionary periods, however, the environment changes significantly. Rising interest rates, inflation concerns, geopolitical instability, slowing economic growth, or declining market confidence can reduce investor appetite for risk. Financing becomes more restrictive, valuation multiples compress, acquisitions slow, and investors prioritize profitability and cash flow stability over aggressive expansion narratives. Businesses dependent entirely on continuous financing often struggle during these cycles because capital suddenly becomes more expensive and selective.

Understanding these cycles allows founders to prepare strategically rather than emotionally. One of the biggest mistakes entrepreneurs make is assuming favorable market conditions will continue indefinitely. Bull markets create confidence, optimism, and aggressive risk-taking behavior. Founders may raise excessive capital, overexpand operations, increase fixed costs, or pursue unsustainable growth assumptions because recent success creates emotional overconfidence. When conditions eventually reverse, businesses lacking financial discipline often face severe pressure.

Sophisticated entrepreneurs think differently. They recognize that economic cycles are natural and inevitable. Rather than building businesses dependent on permanently favorable conditions, they create operational resilience capable of surviving multiple market environments. This often involves maintaining healthy cash reserves, controlling debt exposure carefully, prioritizing scalable cost structures, diversifying revenue streams, and avoiding excessive operational fragility.

Interest rates represent one of the most powerful forces influencing capital markets. Lower interest rates generally encourage investment because borrowing costs decline and investors seek higher returns than fixed-income alternatives can provide. As a result, capital flows more aggressively into equities, venture investments, private equity, technology companies, and growth-oriented assets. Valuation multiples often expand during low-rate environments because future earnings become more attractive relative to safer investments.

Higher interest rates create the opposite effect. Borrowing becomes more expensive, investors become more conservative, and capital often shifts toward safer assets. Valuation multiples frequently contract because future growth becomes less valuable relative to risk-free returns. Businesses dependent on cheap financing may struggle during rising-rate environments, particularly if profitability remains weak.

Founders who understand these dynamics can adjust strategy accordingly. During periods of abundant liquidity and strong investor enthusiasm, companies may accelerate fundraising, acquisitions, expansion initiatives, or public offerings. During tighter monetary conditions, businesses may prioritize cash flow, operational efficiency, debt reduction, and profitability preservation. Timing alone can dramatically influence valuation outcomes and financing terms.

Market sentiment also plays a major role in capital allocation decisions. Financial markets are influenced not only by data but also by psychology, emotion, momentum, and narrative. Investor optimism can drive valuations far above historical norms, while fear can cause sharp market contractions even among fundamentally strong companies. This emotional component explains why market cycles often overshoot in both directions.

The psychology of fear and greed affects nearly every participant within capital markets. During periods of optimism, investors may ignore risk and aggressively pursue speculative opportunities. During downturns, investors may become excessively pessimistic and avoid risk entirely, even when attractive opportunities exist. Sophisticated founders learn how to remain emotionally disciplined while others become reactive.

This emotional discipline becomes especially important during fundraising and liquidity planning. Many founders rush into transactions during periods of market excitement without fully considering long-term implications. Others panic during downturns and accept unfavorable financing terms due to fear or short-term pressure. Entrepreneurs who understand market psychology can often make more rational decisions while competitors react emotionally.

One of the most valuable skills founders can develop is distinguishing between temporary market conditions and long-term structural trends. Economic cycles fluctuate constantly, but certain technological, demographic, and societal trends may continue advancing across multiple cycles. Artificial intelligence, automation, digital infrastructure, healthcare innovation, cybersecurity, renewable energy, creator economies, and global connectivity represent examples of structural trends that continue evolving despite short-term economic volatility.

Businesses aligned with strong long-term trends often recover more quickly after downturns because investor demand eventually returns to sectors perceived as strategically important. Founders who position companies within durable growth themes may therefore maintain stronger long-term optionality even during difficult market environments.

Liquidity cycles also influence merger and acquisition activity significantly. During periods of abundant capital availability, strategic buyers and private equity firms often compete aggressively for acquisitions. Financing becomes easier, valuations increase, and transaction volume rises substantially. During tighter economic periods, acquisition activity may slow as financing becomes more restrictive and buyers grow more cautious. This cyclical behavior creates strategic opportunities for disciplined companies. Businesses with strong balance sheets and healthy cash flow may pursue acquisitions aggressively during downturns when competitors struggle financially and valuations decline. Some of the most successful long-term companies expanded significantly during recessions because they possessed the financial flexibility to act while others retreated.

Public markets exhibit similar cyclical behavior. IPO windows open and close based on investor sentiment, liquidity conditions, and market momentum. During strong IPO environments, investors may reward growth stories aggressively and provide favorable pricing conditions for newly public companies. During weak markets, even fundamentally strong businesses may postpone public offerings because investor demand becomes insufficient.

Sophisticated founders monitor these conditions continuously rather than assuming liquidity opportunities will always remain available. Companies that prepare operationally before favorable market windows emerge often gain significant advantages because they can move quickly when conditions align.

Another important concept is capital rotation. Investors constantly move money between sectors, asset classes, and investment themes based on changing expectations. During certain periods, technology companies may attract enormous investor enthusiasm. During other cycles, investors may favor energy, healthcare, infrastructure, financial services, or defensive industries. Understanding where capital is flowing helps founders anticipate valuation trends and investor priorities.

Global events also influence capital flows significantly. Geopolitical tensions, regulatory changes, trade policies, supply chain disruptions, pandemics, and international conflicts can alter investor behavior rapidly. Modern capital markets are highly interconnected, meaning global uncertainty often affects financing conditions worldwide.

Founders who understand macroeconomic relationships can often interpret these shifts more effectively than competitors focused only on internal operations. This does not require predicting every economic event accurately. Instead, it involves maintaining strategic awareness and preserving flexibility under changing conditions.

One of the greatest advantages a founder can possess during uncertain markets is strong liquidity. Cash provides optionality. Businesses with strong cash reserves can survive downturns more comfortably, negotiate from positions of strength, pursue acquisitions opportunistically, and avoid accepting unfavorable financing terms under pressure. Liquidity creates psychological confidence because the company is not forced into reactive decisions.

Operational flexibility matters equally. Businesses with lean cost structures, scalable systems, recurring revenue, and adaptable infrastructure generally navigate volatility more effectively than companies burdened by excessive fixed costs or operational complexity. Resilience itself becomes a competitive advantage during difficult cycles.

Investor psychology toward leadership also changes across economic environments. During strong markets, investors may prioritize visionary growth narratives aggressively. During downturns, investors often favor disciplined operators capable of preserving capital and managing risk carefully. Founders who can demonstrate both ambition and discipline often maintain stronger long-term credibility across multiple market cycles.

The media plays a major role in shaping investor sentiment as well. Financial news, analyst opinions, social media narratives, and public commentary influence how markets perceive industries and companies. Sophisticated founders understand that perception affects capital access, even when underlying fundamentals remain strong. This does not mean entrepreneurs should become obsessed with short-term market movements. Long-term wealth creation still depends primarily on building fundamentally strong businesses with scalable economics, strong leadership, operational discipline, and strategic positioning. However, understanding market cycles allows founders to align major decisions with favorable conditions whenever possible.

Patience becomes extremely valuable within capital markets strategy. Some founders rush liquidity events prematurely because of ego, fear, or short-term pressure. Others wait too long and miss optimal market windows. Sophisticated entrepreneurs balance preparation with timing awareness. They build businesses capable of acting quickly when opportunities emerge while remaining resilient enough to delay transactions during weak conditions.

Ultimately, advanced capital markets strategy requires combining operational excellence with macroeconomic awareness. Businesses do not create value solely through internal execution. They also create value through intelligent positioning within larger financial systems shaped by human psychology, monetary policy, investor behavior, and economic cycles.

The entrepreneurs who create extraordinary long-term wealth are usually those who remain disciplined while others become emotional. They prepare during calm periods, preserve flexibility during uncertainty, and act decisively when favorable opportunities emerge. They understand that capital flows constantly across markets, and the businesses best positioned to capture those flows often achieve extraordinary outcomes.

Economic cycles are unavoidable, but they do not need to be feared. For disciplined founders, cycles create opportunities as well as risks. Understanding how money moves through the financial system transforms the way entrepreneurs think about growth, financing, valuation, and long-term wealth creation.

The future belongs to founders who combine operational strength with financial intelligence. Businesses that survive multiple economic cycles while maintaining strategic flexibility often emerge stronger, more valuable, and better positioned for transformational liquidity events over time.

The Founder Who Built During the Storm

Ethan Brooks launched his commercial real estate technology company during one of the strongest economic expansions in recent history. Capital flowed easily, investors aggressively funded startups, and nearly every technology conference celebrated endless growth opportunities. Interest rates remained low, venture capital firms competed fiercely for deals, and founders across the country believed the good times would continue indefinitely.

At first, Ethan felt unstoppable.

His company developed software that helped commercial property owners analyze tenant risk, automate leasing workflows, and predict market demand patterns using artificial intelligence. Investors loved the concept because real estate technology had become one of the hottest sectors in the market.

Within eighteen months, Ethan raised millions in venture financing at valuations that seemed almost surreal. Advisors encouraged him to "scale as fast as possible." Competitors raised even larger rounds, hired aggressively, and flooded the market with marketing campaigns.

For a while, everything worked.

Revenue grew rapidly. Industry publications featured Ethan constantly. Employees celebrated funding announcements as if they were victories themselves. Investors encouraged expansion into multiple international markets simultaneously.

But beneath the excitement, Ethan noticed something that troubled him.

Very few companies in the sector were profitable. Most competitors survived entirely on continuous investor financing. Businesses hired aggressively without operational discipline because capital remained abundant. Revenue mattered, but profitability and efficiency seemed almost irrelevant during the boom.

One evening, Ethan visited his grandfather, Samuel, who had spent decades building manufacturing businesses through multiple recessions.

Ethan enthusiastically described the company's growth and recent valuation increase.

Samuel listened quietly before asking one question.

"What happens if the money stops flowing?"

Ethan laughed initially.

"Why would it stop?" he asked.

Samuel smiled carefully.

"Because it always does eventually."

At the time, Ethan dismissed the warning.

But months later, everything changed.

Inflation surged globally. Central banks raised interest rates aggressively. Public technology stocks collapsed. Venture funding slowed dramatically. Investors who had once prioritized growth at all costs suddenly demanded profitability, efficiency, and financial discipline.

The market turned almost overnight.

Competitors began laying off employees aggressively. Several high-profile startups failed entirely after investors refused additional financing. Valuations across the sector collapsed. Fear replaced optimism throughout the investment community.

Ethan felt panic spreading through his executive team.

Employees worried constantly about layoffs. Investors pressured management to reduce spending immediately. News headlines predicted severe recession risks. Companies that once seemed invincible suddenly appeared fragile.

For the first time, Ethan understood what his grandfather had meant.

Capital had stopped flowing.

Fortunately, months earlier, Samuel's warning had affected Ethan more deeply than he initially realized. Quietly, Ethan had already begun strengthening the company's financial position before conditions deteriorated fully. He slowed unnecessary hiring, reduced excessive marketing expenditures, improved operational efficiency, and preserved cash reserves more aggressively than competitors.

At the time, some investors criticized his caution.

Now that caution became the company's survival advantage.

While competitors scrambled desperately for financing, Ethan's company maintained strong liquidity and recurring revenue. The business still faced pressure, but it was not fighting for survival.

Then Ethan made a decision that shocked many advisors.

Instead of retreating completely during the downturn, he began acquiring distressed competitors.

Several struggling companies possessed excellent technology and talented employees but lacked sufficient cash reserves to survive the market contraction. Because Ethan's company remained financially stable, acquisition opportunities appeared at dramatically reduced valuations.

Over the next two years, Ethan completed multiple strategic acquisitions while competitors collapsed around him.

The experience transformed his understanding of capital markets permanently. During boom periods, everyone appeared intelligent because money flowed easily. But during downturns, discipline mattered more than excitement. Businesses with strong fundamentals, liquidity, and operational resilience survived while fragile growth models failed.

As economic conditions gradually stabilized, Ethan's company emerged dramatically stronger than before. Market share increased substantially because many competitors no longer existed. Investors once again became interested in real estate technology, but now they prioritized financially disciplined companies rather than reckless expansion.

Suddenly, Ethan's business stood out.

The company had survived the downturn while expanding strategically. Margins improved, acquisitions strengthened infrastructure, and recurring revenue remained healthy. Institutional investors began viewing the company as one of the strongest operators within the entire sector.

Several years later, investment bankers approached Ethan about a potential IPO.

This time, Ethan viewed market conditions differently.

He no longer assumed favorable environments would last forever. Instead, he analyzed interest rates, investor sentiment, liquidity conditions, and public market comparables carefully before making decisions. The company eventually went public during a period of improving market optimism and strong investor demand for profitable technology platforms.

The IPO became highly successful.

Financial media praised Ethan for "visionary leadership during turbulent economic conditions." But privately, Ethan understood the deeper truth.

The company had not succeeded because he predicted markets perfectly.

It succeeded because he learned how to survive cycles intelligently.

Months after the IPO, Ethan visited his grandfather again.

Samuel sat quietly on the porch while Ethan described the public offering and the company's valuation.

After Ethan finished speaking, Samuel smiled.

"So," he asked calmly, "what did you learn?"

Ethan laughed softly.

"That money moves in cycles," he said. "And businesses built only for good times eventually break."

Samuel nodded.

"Exactly."

Ethan paused before continuing.

"The strongest companies aren't the ones that grow fastest during booms," he said. "They're the ones still standing when the cycle changes."

Samuel smiled proudly.

Now Ethan finally understood the lesson completely.

Capital markets rewarded discipline far more than excitement over the long run.

Chapter 6

IPOs, Acquisitions, and Designing the Perfect Exit Strategy

For many entrepreneurs, building a successful business eventually leads to one critical question: how and when should ownership be converted into long-term personal wealth? This question sits at the center of advanced capital markets strategy because the structure, timing, and execution of an exit event can dramatically influence not only valuation outcomes but also taxes, control, legacy, future opportunities, and generational wealth creation. While many founders dream about “selling the company” or “going public,” relatively few fully understand the complexity behind liquidity events and how sophisticated entrepreneurs intentionally design exit strategies years before transactions occur.

An exit strategy is not simply the act of leaving a business. It is a long-term financial and strategic plan that determines how ownership value will eventually be monetized, transferred, expanded, or preserved. Sophisticated founders understand that exits are rarely single isolated events. Instead, they often unfold in stages over time through partial liquidity, recapitalizations, acquisitions, secondary sales, public offerings, strategic partnerships, or long-term dividend structures. Entrepreneurs who understand these mechanics can dramatically increase both financial outcomes and personal flexibility.

The traditional initial public offering remains one of the most recognized liquidity pathways in modern capital markets. An IPO allows a private company to become publicly traded by offering shares to institutional and retail investors through public exchanges. For many founders, an IPO represents validation, visibility, and access to enormous pools of capital. Public companies may use stock as currency for acquisitions, expansion initiatives, executive compensation, and future fundraising opportunities. Public listings can also increase brand recognition, market influence, and institutional credibility dramatically.

However, IPOs are far more complex than most entrepreneurs realize. Going public introduces extensive regulatory obligations, shareholder expectations, quarterly reporting pressure, public scrutiny, governance requirements, and market volatility. Founders who romanticize IPOs without understanding these responsibilities often become overwhelmed after entering public markets. An IPO should therefore be viewed not as an endpoint but as the beginning of an entirely different operational and financial environment. Preparation for a successful IPO usually begins years before the actual transaction occurs. Public market investors expect audited financial statements, strong governance systems, scalable operations, experienced management teams, legal compliance infrastructure, predictable reporting procedures, and institutional-quality operational controls. Businesses that wait until the final stages to build these systems often encounter costly delays, valuation reductions, or failed offerings.

Another important factor influencing IPO success is public market storytelling. Public investors buy future expectations as much as current performance. Companies capable of communicating compelling long-term growth narratives often attract stronger investor demand and higher valuation multiples. This is why IPO roadshows, investor presentations, analyst relationships, and media positioning become critically important during public offerings.

Yet IPOs are not always the optimal exit path.

Strategic acquisitions remain one of the most common and potentially lucrative liquidity events for business owners. In a strategic acquisition, a larger corporation purchases a company because the target business provides strategic value beyond standalone financial performance. This value may come from technology, market share, intellectual property, customer relationships, operational capabilities, geographic expansion, talent acquisition, or competitive positioning.

Strategic buyers often pay premium valuations because acquisitions may create synergies that improve profitability after integration. For example, a large corporation may acquire a smaller technology company not only for current revenue but also because the technology enhances the buyer's existing infrastructure or eliminates future competition. Businesses possessing strategic value within larger industry ecosystems often command higher acquisition premiums than purely financial buyers would offer.

Private equity acquisitions represent another major category of exits. Unlike strategic buyers, private equity firms usually focus more heavily on operational improvement, financial engineering, scalability, and future resale opportunities. These firms may acquire businesses entirely or purchase majority stakes while retaining founders within leadership roles. Many founders prefer private equity transactions because they often allow partial liquidity while maintaining ongoing operational involvement and future upside participation.

Recapitalizations offer another sophisticated liquidity pathway. In a recapitalization, founders may refinance the business using debt or institutional investment, allowing them to extract partial liquidity while continuing ownership and operational control. This approach reduces pressure for immediate full exits and allows entrepreneurs to participate in future valuation growth. Some founders complete multiple recapitalizations over time while gradually diversifying personal wealth.

Secondary sales have also become increasingly important within modern capital markets. Founders and early investors no longer need to wait exclusively for acquisitions or IPOs to create liquidity. Secondary transactions allow ownership shares to be sold privately to institutional buyers while the company remains private. This flexibility can dramatically reduce founder financial pressure and allow businesses to pursue longer-term strategic growth without rushing toward premature exits.

Management buyouts and employee ownership transitions represent additional exit possibilities. In some situations, founders may gradually transfer ownership to management teams or employees through structured financing arrangements or employee stock ownership plans. These approaches may preserve company culture and legacy while still creating meaningful liquidity for founders.

Family succession planning represents another unique category of exit strategy. Some entrepreneurs prioritize preserving family ownership across generations rather than maximizing short-term liquidity. However, family transitions require careful planning related to governance, taxation, leadership development, operational continuity, and wealth distribution. Poor succession planning has destroyed many otherwise successful businesses over time.

One of the most important principles in exit planning is understanding that valuation is not the only variable that matters. Founders often become overly focused on headline purchase prices while ignoring deal structure, tax implications, liquidity timelines, earn-out provisions, equity rollover requirements, governance restrictions, and post-transaction obligations. Sophisticated entrepreneurs evaluate transactions holistically rather than emotionally.

Taxes can dramatically affect net proceeds after liquidity events occur. Capital gains taxes, ordinary income treatment, state taxation, estate planning issues, international tax considerations, and trust structures all influence how much wealth founders ultimately retain. Many entrepreneurs spend years building valuable businesses only to lose substantial wealth due to poor tax planning before exits occur.

This is why advanced founders work closely with experienced attorneys, accountants, investment bankers, estate planners, and tax advisors long before liquidity events take place. Strategic planning often begins years in advance because certain structures require time to implement effectively.

Emotional psychology also plays a major role during exit decisions. Many founders underestimate how deeply personal identity becomes connected to business ownership. Selling or transitioning a company can create emotional uncertainty even after enormous financial success. Entrepreneurs who have spent decades building organizations may suddenly feel loss of purpose, control, routine, or identity after exits occur.

This emotional reality explains why some founders continue leading companies after acquisitions or public offerings while others struggle significantly after stepping away. Sophisticated exit planning therefore includes not only financial preparation but also personal vision planning for life after liquidity events.

Timing remains critically important throughout exit strategy design. Economic cycles, industry momentum, investor sentiment, public market conditions, interest rates, and acquisition activity all influence valuation outcomes significantly. Some founders exit during periods of peak market enthusiasm and achieve extraordinary premiums. Others delay too long and miss favorable windows entirely.

The best entrepreneurs prepare businesses continuously so they can act quickly when favorable conditions emerge. Businesses that are always "exit-ready" possess stronger flexibility because they can pursue opportunities opportunistically rather than reactively. Exit readiness itself becomes a strategic advantage.

Another important consideration involves retaining future upside. Some founders sell companies entirely and exit completely. Others intentionally retain equity stakes, board positions, advisory roles, or earn-out structures tied to future performance. Partial exits may create substantial wealth while still allowing participation in future growth opportunities.

Public market founders often use staged liquidity strategies. Rather than selling all shares immediately after IPOs, they may gradually diversify holdings over time while preserving long-term ownership exposure. This approach balances liquidity creation with future upside participation.

The relationship between wealth creation and wealth preservation becomes especially important after exits occur. Many entrepreneurs excel at building businesses but struggle with managing large pools of capital afterward. Sudden wealth introduces entirely new financial complexities involving diversification, investment management, philanthropy, estate planning, family governance, tax strategy, and long-term legacy planning. Some founders become overly concentrated in their own company stock and experience major wealth destruction during market downturns. Others overspend impulsively after liquidity events without building sustainable long-term financial structures. Sophisticated entrepreneurs recognize that liquidity events are transitions into entirely new financial phases requiring different expertise and discipline.

Legacy planning also becomes increasingly important as wealth expands. Many founders eventually focus not only on personal wealth but also on generational impact, philanthropy, family governance, educational opportunities, and community influence. Businesses can become platforms for much larger long-term missions beyond simple financial success.

One of the greatest misconceptions about exit strategy is that there exists one perfect pathway for all entrepreneurs. In reality, optimal exit structures vary dramatically depending on industry, market conditions, founder goals, family circumstances, operational readiness, investor relationships, and long-term vision. The best exit strategy is the one aligned intelligently with both financial objectives and personal priorities.

Sophisticated founders therefore design businesses with optionality in mind. They preserve flexibility so companies remain attractive to multiple future pathways including acquisitions, IPOs, recapitalizations, strategic partnerships, or continued private ownership. Optionality increases negotiating leverage and allows founders to adapt strategically as conditions evolve.

The most successful entrepreneurs understand that exits are not simply financial transactions. They are carefully engineered strategic events shaped by years of operational preparation, financial discipline, market awareness, legal structuring, emotional maturity, and long-term planning. The founders who create extraordinary outcomes are usually those who think about exits early, prepare continuously, and remain flexible enough to capitalize on opportunities when timing aligns.

Ultimately, advanced capital markets strategy is about more than building businesses. It is about designing ownership structures and liquidity pathways capable of transforming entrepreneurial effort into long-term financial freedom, family security, and lasting impact.

The future belongs to founders who understand how to create value, preserve value, and eventually convert value into sustainable wealth intelligently. Businesses may generate opportunity, but carefully designed exits determine how much of that opportunity becomes permanent long-term prosperity.

The Exit That Almost Didn't Happen

Nathan Cole never planned to sell his company.

When he launched his cybersecurity software business at age twenty-nine, his only goal was survival. He had left a stable corporate technology job after growing frustrated with outdated security systems used by midsize financial institutions. Convinced that artificial intelligence would transform cybersecurity, Nathan built a platform capable of detecting suspicious transaction patterns in real time.

The early years were brutal.

Banks moved slowly, investors were skeptical, and larger competitors dismissed the company as insignificant. Nathan maxed out credit cards, borrowed money from relatives, and worked nearly every day for years. Several times he considered shutting the business down entirely.

But gradually, the technology improved.

A few regional banks adopted the platform first. Then several national institutions signed contracts after experiencing major fraud prevention improvements. Recurring revenue grew steadily, and the company developed a reputation for innovation within the financial security industry. By year eight, the business had become one of the fastest-growing private cybersecurity firms in the country.

That was when acquisition offers began arriving.

At first, Nathan ignored them completely. He still viewed the company emotionally rather than strategically. The business represented years of sacrifice, stress, identity, and personal struggle. Selling felt almost like abandoning a part of himself.

His executive team disagreed.

"Large institutions are entering the market aggressively," warned his COO, Melissa. "Competition is changing fast."

Nathan resisted.

"We're still growing," he argued. "Why would we sell now?"

But the market environment kept evolving. Large technology conglomerates began consolidating cybersecurity firms rapidly. Private equity money flooded into the sector. Competitors raised massive institutional rounds and expanded internationally.

Then one morning, Nathan received a call from a global financial technology corporation.

The CEO wanted a meeting immediately. Over the next several weeks, discussions intensified. The corporation viewed Nathan's platform as strategically valuable because it could integrate directly into their existing global banking infrastructure. Internally, executives estimated the acquisition could strengthen billions of dollars in financial transaction systems worldwide.

The valuation discussions became enormous.

Far larger than Nathan had ever imagined possible.

Yet strangely, Nathan felt anxious instead of excited.

One evening, he sat alone in his office reviewing acquisition documents while staring at the city skyline outside the window. The company had become his life. Employees felt like family. The thought of losing control terrified him.

That night, he called his mentor, Richard, a retired founder who had completed multiple major exits throughout his career.

Nathan explained his fears honestly.

Richard listened quietly before asking a simple question.

"What exactly are you afraid of losing?"

Nathan paused.

"Purpose," he admitted eventually. Richard nodded slowly.

"That's the real challenge," he said. "Most founders think exits are financial decisions. They're emotional decisions disguised as financial transactions."

The conversation changed Nathan's perspective completely.

Over the next several months, Nathan stopped focusing only on the purchase price. Instead, he began analyzing the entire structure strategically. He hired experienced advisors specializing in tax planning, mergers, wealth management, and post-acquisition transitions.

For the first time, Nathan realized how many founders destroyed wealth by focusing only on headline valuations.

Taxes alone could dramatically alter final outcomes. Earn-out structures created hidden risks. Stock compensation components exposed founders to future market volatility. Governance terms affected operational control after closing.

Nathan negotiated carefully.

Rather than accepting a full cash acquisition and immediate

departure, he structured a hybrid transaction. He sold a majority stake for significant liquidity while retaining meaningful equity exposure tied to future platform expansion. He also negotiated continued leadership authority over the cybersecurity division for several years following the acquisition.

The structure changed everything psychologically.

Nathan no longer viewed the transaction as an ending.

It became a transition.

When the acquisition finally closed, media headlines celebrated the deal as one of the largest cybersecurity acquisitions of the decade. Financial commentators praised Nathan as a visionary entrepreneur who had transformed banking security infrastructure.

But privately, Nathan knew the deeper lesson.

The success of the exit came not from luck or timing alone.

It came from preparation.

Because he had built scalable systems, recurring revenue, institutional reporting structures, and strategic market positioning years earlier, the company became highly valuable within the broader capital markets ecosystem.

Even more importantly, Nathan had learned how to separate emotion from structure during negotiations. Years later, Nathan managed a family investment office overseeing multiple businesses, venture investments, philanthropic initiatives, and technology incubators. He still advised cybersecurity startups occasionally, but his relationship with business had evolved dramatically.

One afternoon, a young founder asked him whether selling his company had been the happiest moment of his life.

Nathan smiled thoughtfully.

"No," he answered honestly. "Building it was harder. But understanding how to exit intelligently changed my life forever."

The founder looked confused.

Nathan leaned forward slightly.

"Most entrepreneurs spend years learning how to start businesses," he explained. "Very few spend enough time learning how to leave them."

The room became quiet.

Nathan continued.

"If you don't design the exit carefully, you can spend decades building wealth and still lose control of your future."

The founder asked what mattered most. Nathan smiled.

"Optionality," he said. "Always build your company so you have choices when opportunity arrives."

Then he paused.

"Because the perfect exit is rarely about selling everything," he added. "It's about creating freedom without destroying the future you worked so hard to build."

Chapter 7

Building Generational Wealth Through Equity, Ownership, and Long-Term Capital Allocation

The ultimate purpose of advanced capital markets strategy extends far beyond achieving a successful exit or accumulating short-term financial wealth. True financial mastery involves transforming temporary business success into sustainable, multigenerational prosperity capable of creating opportunity, stability, influence, and long-term freedom for decades to come. Many entrepreneurs spend years building highly valuable companies only to lose substantial portions of their wealth due to poor capital allocation, emotional decision-making, tax inefficiencies, lack of diversification, family conflict, or inadequate long-term planning. Building wealth and preserving wealth require completely different skill sets. Entrepreneurs who understand this distinction position themselves not only to create financial success but also to protect and multiply it across generations.

One of the most important principles in long-term wealth creation is understanding the power of ownership. Wealthy individuals rarely depend entirely on labor income. Instead, they accumulate ownership in appreciating assets such as businesses, equities, intellectual property, real estate, cash-flowing investments, infrastructure, private companies, and scalable financial systems. Ownership allows capital to compound over time independently from direct labor. This compounding effect becomes one of the most powerful forces in financial growth because assets continue generating returns while increasing in value simultaneously.

Equity ownership represents one of the greatest wealth-building tools ever created. Founders who retain meaningful ownership stakes in scalable businesses often generate wealth exponentially larger than what could be achieved through salary or consulting income alone. This is because enterprise value can grow far faster than personal labor capacity. A founder may work the same number of hours annually while the value of the company increases by tens or hundreds of millions of dollars due to scalability, market expansion, investor demand, or operational leverage.

This principle explains why so many of the world's wealthiest individuals built fortunes through equity rather than compensation. Ownership creates asymmetrical upside. If a business scales successfully, the value of ownership may expand dramatically while operational costs grow much more slowly. Entrepreneurs who understand this concept focus less on maximizing immediate personal income and more on building scalable enterprise value capable of compounding over long periods.

However, ownership alone is not enough. Long-term wealth preservation requires disciplined capital allocation. Capital allocation refers to how financial resources are deployed after liquidity events occur. Sophisticated wealth builders understand that money must continue working strategically after exits rather than remaining idle or being consumed through excessive lifestyle inflation.

Many entrepreneurs make the mistake of increasing spending dramatically after major liquidity events. Luxury homes, vehicles, travel, speculative investments, and oversized lifestyles often consume wealth faster than expected. Without disciplined investment structures, even substantial fortunes can deteriorate surprisingly quickly over time. History contains countless examples of entrepreneurs, athletes, entertainers, and lottery winners who accumulated enormous wealth temporarily but failed to preserve it long term.

Sophisticated capital allocators think differently. They prioritize asset acquisition over consumption. Instead of focusing primarily on lifestyle expansion, they deploy capital into investments capable of generating future cash flow, appreciation, and optionality. Businesses, real estate portfolios, dividend-producing equities, private investments, intellectual property, and infrastructure assets become tools for compounding wealth across decades.

Diversification plays a critical role in wealth preservation. Many founders remain excessively concentrated in a single company or industry even after achieving liquidity opportunities. While concentration often creates wealth initially, excessive concentration can also destroy wealth rapidly during market downturns or operational disruptions. Sophisticated entrepreneurs gradually diversify holdings across multiple asset classes, industries, geographic regions, and investment structures in order to reduce long-term risk exposure.

This does not mean abandoning conviction or entrepreneurial ambition. Instead, it means recognizing that wealth preservation requires balancing upside potential with resilience. Financial independence becomes much more sustainable when multiple independent income streams and asset categories support long-term stability.

Real estate has historically played a major role in generational wealth creation because it combines appreciation potential, leverage opportunities, cash flow generation, inflation protection, and tax advantages. Many successful entrepreneurs allocate portions of liquidity proceeds into commercial real estate, multifamily properties, industrial assets, land development, or income-producing portfolios capable of generating recurring long-term revenue.

Private equity investing also becomes increasingly important as wealth expands. Founders who successfully exit businesses often reinvest capital into emerging companies, venture funds, acquisition opportunities, or private investment partnerships. These investments can create additional exponential upside while leveraging entrepreneurial experience and industry knowledge.

Public equities remain another major wealth-building vehicle. Ownership of high-quality publicly traded companies allows investors to participate in long-term economic growth while maintaining liquidity and diversification. Sophisticated wealth builders often combine private investments with public market exposure in order to balance growth potential and financial flexibility.

One of the most overlooked aspects of long-term wealth strategy involves taxes. Tax planning dramatically influences how much wealth families ultimately retain over generations. Capital gains taxes, estate taxes, inheritance structures, trust planning, charitable foundations, family limited partnerships, insurance structures, and geographic residency decisions all affect long-term wealth preservation outcomes.

Families that fail to plan strategically often lose enormous percentages of wealth during generational transitions. By contrast, sophisticated family offices work closely with estate attorneys, tax strategists, accountants, and investment advisors to create structures designed for multigenerational continuity.

Trusts represent one of the most important tools within long-term wealth preservation. Properly structured trusts can help protect assets, reduce tax exposure, preserve privacy, support charitable initiatives, and create financial stability for future generations. However, trust structures must be designed carefully based on family goals, jurisdictional laws, and long-term financial strategy.

Philanthropy also becomes increasingly important as wealth expands. Many entrepreneurs eventually shift focus from personal accumulation toward impact creation. Charitable foundations, donor-advised funds, educational initiatives, healthcare programs, community investment projects, and social enterprises become vehicles for long-term legacy building. Strategic philanthropy can create both societal impact and tax efficiency simultaneously. Another major challenge within generational wealth planning involves family governance. Financial wealth alone does not guarantee long-term family success. Many wealthy families lose fortunes within two or three generations due to poor communication, entitlement, lack of financial education, emotional conflict, or absence of shared vision. Sustainable wealth preservation requires teaching future generations about responsibility, capital allocation, ownership, and stewardship.

This is why some wealthy families establish family constitutions, governance councils, investment education programs, and long-term mission frameworks designed to preserve values alongside financial assets. The goal is not simply transferring money. The goal is transferring wisdom, discipline, and strategic thinking.

Psychology plays an enormous role in long-term wealth outcomes. Sudden wealth can create emotional instability, impulsive decision-making, social pressure, and identity confusion. Some entrepreneurs struggle after exits because the process of building companies provided structure, competition, and purpose. Without meaningful long-term vision, wealth itself may become psychologically destabilizing.

Sophisticated wealth creators therefore maintain purpose beyond money. They continue building businesses, mentoring entrepreneurs, investing strategically, supporting charitable causes, or pursuing long-term missions aligned with personal values. Wealth becomes a tool for freedom and impact rather than simply consumption.

Inflation awareness is another critical factor in generational planning. Cash alone rarely preserves purchasing power effectively over long periods. Wealth must remain invested in productive assets capable of growing faster than inflation over time. Businesses, equities, real estate, and infrastructure often provide stronger long-term protection than idle cash reserves alone.

Global diversification also becomes increasingly important within modern wealth strategy. Economic cycles, political changes, currency fluctuations, and regulatory shifts vary across regions. International diversification through businesses, investments, real estate, and banking structures can reduce concentrated geographic risk while expanding opportunity access.

Another key principle in generational wealth creation is patience. Compounding works most powerfully across long time horizons. Many wealthy families achieve extraordinary outcomes not through short-term speculation but through disciplined multi-decade ownership of appreciating assets. Time itself becomes one of the greatest wealth-building advantages available to patient investors.

Technology and innovation continue reshaping wealth creation opportunities rapidly. Artificial intelligence, digital infrastructure, blockchain systems, biotechnology, cybersecurity, renewable energy, creator economies, and automation platforms are creating entirely new categories of scalable assets. Entrepreneurs who remain adaptable and forward-thinking may continue compounding wealth across multiple technological eras.

One of the most valuable concepts in advanced capital allocation is optionality. Wealth creates freedom because it expands strategic choices. Financial independence allows entrepreneurs to pursue opportunities selectively rather than reactively. Optionality reduces desperation and increases negotiating leverage across nearly every aspect of life and business.

This is why sophisticated entrepreneurs focus heavily on liquidity management. Illiquid wealth can create vulnerability even when net worth appears substantial on paper. Maintaining balanced liquidity allows families to survive downturns, pursue investments opportunistically, support future ventures, and navigate uncertainty without being forced into unfavorable decisions. Legacy eventually becomes the central question for many successful entrepreneurs. Financial wealth alone rarely creates lasting fulfillment. Most founders eventually begin asking deeper questions about contribution, impact, family continuity, and long-term meaning. Businesses may generate capital, but legacy determines how that capital influences future generations and society itself.

The greatest wealth builders understand that money represents stored opportunity. Capital can create businesses, fund innovation, support families, improve communities, expand educational access, accelerate healthcare solutions, and generate freedom across generations. Wealth therefore becomes much more than personal success. It becomes a strategic resource capable of shaping future outcomes at scale.

Ultimately, advanced capital markets strategy is not simply about achieving liquidity events or maximizing short-term valuations. It is about learning how ownership, discipline, capital allocation, diversification, governance, and long-term thinking combine to create enduring prosperity.

The entrepreneurs who create lasting multigenerational wealth are usually those who understand both creation and preservation simultaneously. They build aggressively, invest intelligently, diversify strategically, educate continuously, and remain emotionally disciplined regardless of market cycles. The future belongs not only to founders who build valuable companies but also to those who learn how to transform temporary business success into permanent long-term financial freedom and enduring generational opportunity.

The Family Office

When Anthony Russo sold his industrial automation company at age fifty-two, the financial world called him a genius.

The acquisition valued his company at nearly $900 million, instantly transforming Anthony into one of the wealthiest entrepreneurs in the region. Financial media celebrated the deal relentlessly. Friends congratulated him constantly. Luxury real estate brokers, private bankers, investment advisors, and wealth managers flooded his inbox with invitations and proposals.

For the first few months, Anthony enjoyed the excitement.

He purchased a waterfront estate, upgraded his cars, traveled internationally, and experienced the type of financial freedom he had once considered impossible. After decades of sacrifice and relentless work, he believed he had finally “made it.”

But slowly, something unexpected happened.

The excitement faded.

Anthony realized that building the company had given him structure, challenge, and purpose. Now, despite enormous wealth, he felt strangely unsettled. Worse, he began noticing how quickly money could disappear when handled carelessly.

Friends pitched speculative investments constantly. Family members requested financial help. Luxury expenses escalated rapidly. Advisors pushed complicated financial products that Anthony barely understood. For the first time in decades, he felt uncertain again.

One evening, while reviewing investment statements, Anthony noticed that several supposedly "safe" investments had already lost substantial value due to market volatility. At the same time, taxes from the acquisition consumed far more wealth than he had anticipated originally.

Suddenly, Anthony realized something important.

Building wealth and managing wealth were completely different skills.

The next morning, he called Eleanor Whitman, a highly respected advisor known for helping entrepreneurial families preserve wealth across generations.

Their first meeting changed Anthony's life. Eleanor asked almost nothing about the acquisition itself. Instead, she focused on deeper questions.

"What do you want your wealth to accomplish?" she asked calmly.

Anthony hesitated.

No one had ever asked him that before.

For decades, his focus had been survival, growth, and eventually the sale. He had never truly considered what came afterward.

Over the following months, Eleanor helped Anthony rethink everything.

Instead of treating wealth as money to spend, she taught him to view capital as a long-term strategic asset. Together, they created a family office structure designed to manage investments, taxes, estate planning, philanthropy, and multigenerational education.

Anthony diversified aggressively.

He invested in real estate portfolios, infrastructure projects, dividend-producing equities, private companies, venture funds, and cash-flowing assets. Rather than chasing speculative opportunities, he focused on long-term compounding and resilience. The transformation extended beyond investments.

Eleanor insisted Anthony involve his children gradually in family governance discussions. At first, Anthony resisted because he feared creating entitlement. But Eleanor explained that wealthy families often failed because they transferred money without transferring financial education or responsibility.

Slowly, family meetings became part of their routine.

Anthony's children learned about investing, taxes, ownership structures, philanthropy, and business operations. Rather than simply inheriting wealth passively one day, they began understanding stewardship and responsibility.

Anthony also established a charitable foundation supporting vocational education and engineering programs for underserved communities. For the first time since selling the company, he felt purpose returning to his life.

Years passed.

Economic cycles came and went. Markets rose and crashed repeatedly. Some investments failed completely, while others performed exceptionally well. But because the family office remained diversified and disciplined, long-term wealth continued compounding steadily.

One afternoon, Anthony attended a private conference for entrepreneurs who had recently sold businesses.

Many attendees looked stressed despite enormous liquidity events. Some had concentrated most of their wealth into risky investments. Others faced family conflict, tax problems, or post-exit depression.

During a panel discussion, one founder asked Anthony what advice he would give entrepreneurs after major exits.

Anthony thought carefully before answering.

"Most founders spend decades learning how to build wealth," he said. "Very few spend enough time learning how to keep it."

The room became quiet.

Anthony continued.

"Wealth disappears surprisingly fast when there's no structure behind it. You need systems, education, diversification, governance, and long-term vision—just like you needed systems to build your company."

After the conference ended, a younger entrepreneur approached Anthony privately.

"What changed everything for you?" the entrepreneur asked. Anthony smiled.

"The moment I realized money itself isn't the goal," he said. "The goal is creating freedom, stability, opportunity, and impact that outlives you."

The entrepreneur nodded thoughtfully.

Anthony looked out across the city skyline through the conference center windows.

Years earlier, he had believed the acquisition itself represented the finish line.

Now he understood it had only been the beginning of a completely different journey.

Chapter 8

The Future of Capital Markets, AI, and the Next Generation of Wealth Creation

The global financial system is entering one of the most transformative periods in modern history. Advances in artificial intelligence, automation, blockchain infrastructure, digital platforms, decentralized finance, global connectivity, cloud computing, predictive analytics, and machine learning are rapidly changing how businesses are built, financed, scaled, valued, and monetized. Entrepreneurs who understand these shifts early may position themselves to create extraordinary wealth opportunities over the coming decades, while those who ignore technological transformation risk becoming obsolete within rapidly evolving markets.

Capital markets have always evolved alongside technological innovation. Railroads transformed industrial finance during the nineteenth century. Telecommunications accelerated global commerce during the twentieth century. The internet revolutionized business scalability and information distribution during the early twenty-first century. Today, artificial intelligence and digital infrastructure are creating another major transition capable of reshaping nearly every aspect of business ownership and capital allocation.

One of the most important shifts occurring today involves the dramatic reduction in barriers to scalability. In previous generations, building large companies often required enormous physical infrastructure, expensive distribution systems, large labor forces, and substantial upfront capital. Modern entrepreneurs can now launch highly scalable digital businesses using cloud infrastructure, AI automation, remote teams, social media distribution, and software platforms with relatively low initial costs compared to traditional industrial businesses.

This transformation has democratized entrepreneurship globally. A small team with the right technology stack can now reach international audiences, automate operations, analyze customer behavior, generate content, process transactions, manage marketing campaigns, and scale products worldwide without requiring the massive infrastructure once necessary for expansion. As a result, wealth creation opportunities have expanded dramatically for founders capable of leveraging modern technology intelligently.

Artificial intelligence sits at the center of this transformation. AI is not simply another software tool. It represents a fundamental shift in productivity, automation, data analysis, customer interaction, operational scalability, and decision-making capabilities. Businesses that integrate AI effectively may achieve operational leverage far beyond traditional business models because intelligent systems can automate tasks that previously required large human workforces.

Customer service automation, predictive analytics, marketing optimization, financial modeling, fraud detection, underwriting analysis, software development, content generation, logistics management, and personalized recommendation systems are just a few examples of areas where AI is already reshaping business economics. Companies capable of implementing AI strategically may reduce costs, improve efficiency, increase scalability, and strengthen competitive positioning simultaneously.

Investors recognize this transformation clearly. Capital has flowed aggressively toward AI-related businesses because markets anticipate long-term structural changes across nearly every industry. However, sophisticated entrepreneurs understand that long-term success requires more than simply adding AI terminology to marketing materials. Sustainable value creation comes from building businesses that genuinely improve efficiency, scalability, and customer outcomes through intelligent technology integration.

One of the most powerful effects of AI involves accelerating operational scalability. Traditionally, scaling businesses required proportionally increasing labor, management complexity, and infrastructure costs. AI-driven systems now allow companies to expand output while maintaining lean operational structures. This operating leverage can significantly increase profit margins and enterprise valuation potential.

The creator economy also represents a major shift within modern capital markets. Individuals can now build global audiences, monetize expertise, create digital products, launch subscription communities, distribute educational platforms, produce media content, and build personal brands independently at massive scale. In many cases, creators effectively become media companies themselves.

This shift has created entirely new asset classes built around audience ownership, digital influence, intellectual property, and online distribution systems. Entrepreneurs who combine expertise, technology, branding, and scalable digital infrastructure can generate recurring revenue streams globally without traditional gatekeepers.

Digital education platforms illustrate this trend clearly. Experts who once taught locally can now distribute courses, coaching systems, memberships, audiobooks, certifications, and digital resources worldwide through online platforms. These businesses often possess high scalability because content can be replicated infinitely at relatively low marginal cost. Subscription models continue reshaping capital markets as well. Investors strongly favor recurring revenue because predictable cash flow increases valuation stability and reduces operational uncertainty. Membership businesses, SaaS platforms, subscription media, recurring consulting retainers, licensing systems, and digital communities all benefit from recurring revenue economics that institutional investors often reward heavily.

Blockchain technology and decentralized finance introduce another layer of transformation. While speculative hype has surrounded portions of the cryptocurrency sector, the underlying technology continues influencing capital markets infrastructure significantly. Smart contracts, tokenized assets, decentralized payment systems, blockchain verification protocols, and digital ownership systems may eventually reshape how transactions, investments, contracts, and financial transfers occur globally.

Tokenization of assets could eventually expand liquidity across previously illiquid markets. Real estate, private company equity, intellectual property rights, collectibles, infrastructure projects, and investment funds may become increasingly divisible and globally tradable through blockchain-based systems. While regulatory frameworks continue evolving, entrepreneurs who understand these trends may identify emerging opportunities early.

Globalization and remote work are also altering how companies scale. Businesses no longer require centralized physical offices or geographically concentrated labor pools in order to build significant enterprise value. Remote teams, global freelancers, AI collaboration tools, and cloud-based operations allow companies to recruit talent internationally while maintaining lean infrastructure costs.

This shift increases competition but also expands opportunity. Entrepreneurs can now access global customer bases and international talent simultaneously. Companies capable of managing distributed systems effectively may scale much faster than traditional location-dependent organizations.

Data has become one of the most valuable assets within modern capital markets. Businesses that collect, organize, analyze, and leverage data intelligently often gain major competitive advantages. Customer behavior analytics, predictive modeling, operational optimization, personalization systems, and machine learning infrastructure all rely heavily on quality data ecosystems.

However, data ownership and privacy concerns are becoming increasingly important as well. Regulatory frameworks related to privacy, cybersecurity, AI ethics, and digital governance continue evolving globally. Businesses capable of balancing innovation with compliance and trust may gain long-term advantages as regulation increases.

Cybersecurity itself has become a critical capital markets issue. As economies become increasingly digitized, cyber threats continue expanding. Businesses capable of protecting digital infrastructure, securing financial systems, and maintaining operational resilience against cyberattacks may command premium valuations because trust and security are essential within digital ecosystems.

Another major trend involves the increasing speed of innovation cycles. Industries now evolve faster than at any previous point in modern history. Businesses that fail to adapt technologically may become obsolete rapidly, while adaptable companies capable of continuous innovation may maintain strong competitive positioning across changing market environments.

This acceleration makes intellectual flexibility increasingly important for entrepreneurs. Founders can no longer rely solely on static business models or past success formulas. Continuous learning, technological awareness, and adaptability become essential long-term survival skills within modern capital markets. The future of wealth creation will likely reward hybrid thinkers—individuals capable of combining entrepreneurship, technology understanding, capital allocation skill, branding, automation, and strategic positioning simultaneously. Traditional industry boundaries continue blurring as software, AI, finance, media, education, healthcare, and commerce become increasingly interconnected.

Artificial intelligence may also transform investment management itself. Predictive analytics, algorithmic trading systems, automated underwriting models, portfolio optimization tools, and AI-driven financial analysis platforms are already reshaping institutional investing. Entrepreneurs who understand how these systems function may gain advantages in fundraising, valuation positioning, and capital allocation.

Personal branding is becoming more financially valuable as well. In an increasingly digital economy, reputation, audience trust, expertise visibility, and online influence may significantly affect business scalability and capital access. Founders who build strong public credibility often attract opportunities more easily because investors, customers, and strategic partners recognize their authority and market influence.

One important cautionary principle, however, is that technology alone does not guarantee durable value creation. Markets eventually reward businesses that solve real problems sustainably rather than simply following trends superficially. Many speculative technology bubbles collapse because hype temporarily exceeds practical utility. Sophisticated entrepreneurs focus on long-term economic fundamentals even while embracing innovation.

Human psychology remains central to capital markets despite technological advances. Fear, greed, optimism, uncertainty, and social behavior continue influencing investment decisions across every market cycle. Entrepreneurs who understand both technology and psychology may possess significant long-term advantages because capital flows are ultimately driven by human expectations about the future.

The speed of information distribution also increases market volatility. Social media, digital news, algorithmic trading, and instant communication can rapidly amplify investor sentiment across markets globally. Businesses must therefore manage reputation, communication, and public perception more carefully than ever before.

Education itself is changing dramatically. Traditional career paths are evolving as automation reshapes labor markets. Entrepreneurship, digital skills, financial literacy, AI understanding, and capital allocation knowledge may become increasingly important forms of economic leverage in the future economy.

The next generation of wealth creators will likely emerge from individuals capable of building scalable digital assets, leveraging automation intelligently, understanding global capital flows, and adapting rapidly to technological change. Geographic limitations matter less than ever before. Intellectual capital, adaptability, and ownership of scalable systems increasingly determine long-term financial outcomes.

Yet despite all technological transformation, certain timeless principles remain constant. Ownership still matters. Scalability still drives valuation. Optionality still creates leverage. Discipline still preserves wealth. Relationships still influence opportunity. Trust still determines long-term sustainability.

Technology changes the tools, but human incentives remain remarkably consistent.

Ultimately, the future of capital markets belongs to entrepreneurs capable of combining innovation with strategic financial intelligence. Businesses that leverage technology while maintaining operational discipline, customer trust, and scalable economics may create extraordinary long-term enterprise value. The coming decades will likely produce some of the largest wealth creation opportunities in modern history for founders who understand how AI, automation, digital infrastructure, and global capital markets are converging simultaneously. Entrepreneurs who position themselves early within these transformations may build companies capable of scaling faster, reaching broader audiences, and generating more leverage than previous generations could have imagined.

The future will reward not only hard work but also adaptability, technological fluency, ownership, strategic positioning, and intelligent capital allocation. The next era of wealth creation has already begun.

The AI Founder

Lucas Bennett never planned to become one of the most talked-about entrepreneurs in the technology industry.

At twenty-seven years old, he lived in a modest apartment while working remotely as a freelance programmer and data analyst. Like many young professionals, Lucas initially viewed artificial intelligence simply as another technical skill that might improve his career opportunities.

But over time, he began noticing something much larger happening.

Businesses everywhere struggled with inefficiency. Customer service teams were overwhelmed. Marketing departments wasted enormous advertising budgets. Mortgage companies processed paperwork manually. Healthcare offices buried employees under repetitive administrative tasks. Small business owners spent endless hours handling operations that software could potentially automate.

Lucas realized AI was not just another technology trend.

It was an infrastructure revolution.

Most importantly, he recognized that AI dramatically reduced the amount of labor required to scale businesses.

One evening, while helping a friend who owned a small insurance brokerage, Lucas built a simple AI-powered system that automatically summarized customer conversations, categorized client needs, and generated follow-up recommendations. What previously required hours of manual administrative work suddenly took minutes.

The insurance broker was stunned.

"You just saved my staff twenty hours a week," he said.

That moment changed Lucas's life.

Over the next year, Lucas built a platform focused on helping small and midsize financial companies automate repetitive operational workflows using AI. The software handled document organization, customer communication analysis, predictive lead scoring, compliance monitoring, and workflow automation simultaneously.

At first, very few investors paid attention.

Some people still viewed AI as overhyped. Others assumed only giant corporations would benefit from automation technology. But Lucas understood something many others missed.

AI would eventually become a productivity layer integrated into nearly every industry.

Instead of targeting massive enterprise clients immediately, Lucas focused on smaller businesses desperate for efficiency improvements. The strategy worked perfectly. Customers adopted the platform rapidly because the software solved immediate operational problems while reducing labor costs significantly.

The company scaled faster than Lucas imagined possible.

Because much of the platform operated through automation and cloud infrastructure, operational costs remained relatively lean even as customer growth accelerated internationally. Revenue became highly recurring because businesses integrated the software deeply into daily workflows. Investors suddenly became interested.

Venture capital firms flooded Lucas with meeting requests. Technology conferences invited him to speak constantly. Journalists described the company as one of the fastest-growing AI infrastructure startups in the market.

But unlike many founders during previous technology booms, Lucas remained cautious.

He studied historical market cycles obsessively. He understood that hype alone could disappear quickly. Instead of focusing only on growth metrics, he prioritized recurring revenue quality, customer retention, operational scalability, and profitability pathways.

Some investors criticized his discipline.

"You should be spending much more aggressively," one venture capitalist argued. "The market is moving fast."

Lucas disagreed.

He wanted durability, not just momentum.

Over the next several years, the company expanded globally. AI automation transformed industries faster than most analysts predicted. Businesses everywhere faced labor shortages, operational inefficiencies, and rising demand for scalable digital infrastructure. Lucas's platform became increasingly valuable because it solved practical business problems rather than chasing hype cycles.

Then something unexpected happened.

Public markets began rewarding profitable AI infrastructure companies far more aggressively than speculative startups. Investors shifted focus toward businesses with real recurring revenue, strong margins, and scalable operational systems.

Suddenly, Lucas's disciplined strategy became a massive advantage.

Investment banks approached him regarding a potential IPO.

The company's valuation projections exceeded billions of dollars.

One evening, Lucas sat alone in the company headquarters after most employees had left. He looked around the office quietly, remembering the tiny apartment where he had first started experimenting with AI workflows years earlier.

The scale of transformation felt surreal.

But what fascinated him most was not the money.

It was the realization that technology had fundamentally changed how wealth could be created.

Previous generations required enormous infrastructure and huge organizations to scale globally. Now a relatively lean company powered by software, automation, and cloud infrastructure could influence industries worldwide within only a few years.

The barriers had changed completely.

When the company eventually went public, financial media celebrated Lucas as one of the leading entrepreneurs of the AI revolution. Investors praised the company's scalable infrastructure and operational leverage. Universities invited him to lecture about the future of entrepreneurship.

During one interview, a journalist asked Lucas what made the modern economy different from previous generations.

Lucas thought carefully before answering.

"Technology has compressed scale," he explained. "A small group of people with the right systems can now build companies that once required massive corporations."

The journalist asked whether AI would eliminate entrepreneurship or increase opportunity.

Lucas smiled. "AI won't replace entrepreneurs," he said. "It will amplify the entrepreneurs who understand how to use leverage."

The interviewer asked him what type of people would create the most wealth in the future.

Lucas answered immediately.

"The people who combine ownership, adaptability, technology, and capital allocation," he said. "The tools are changing fast, but the principles of leverage are becoming even more important."

As the interview ended, Lucas looked out across the city skyline through the studio window.

He knew the world was only at the beginning of the transformation.

And he also knew that the next generation of wealth creators would not simply work harder.

They would build smarter systems capable of scaling far beyond themselves.

Chapter 9

Building an Empire Mindset — From Entrepreneur to Capital Allocator

Most entrepreneurs begin their journeys focused on survival. The early stages of business ownership usually revolve around generating revenue, acquiring customers, managing operations, paying expenses, and maintaining stability. Founders often wear multiple roles simultaneously while sacrificing time, energy, and financial security in pursuit of growth. During this stage, the entrepreneur functions primarily as an operator. The business depends heavily on direct effort, daily involvement, and constant decision-making. However, as companies scale and wealth expands, the individuals who create extraordinary long-term fortunes eventually undergo a fundamental transformation in thinking. They stop viewing themselves only as business owners and begin operating as capital allocators.

This transition represents one of the most important mindset shifts in advanced capital markets strategy. Operators focus primarily on working inside businesses. Capital allocators focus on deploying resources strategically across multiple assets, industries, opportunities, and systems designed to compound wealth over time. The entrepreneur builds the machine. The capital allocator decides where the machine's profits should flow in order to maximize long-term value creation.

Many founders never make this transition successfully. Even after achieving significant wealth, they continue operating from a scarcity mindset rooted in earlier survival stages. They remain emotionally attached to controlling every operational detail, overconcentrate wealth in single businesses, or fail to think strategically about long-term capital deployment. As a result, they may achieve temporary financial success without building sustainable financial empires.

Empire thinking requires a broader perspective. Instead of focusing on isolated transactions or individual businesses, sophisticated capital allocators build interconnected ecosystems of assets capable of reinforcing one another over decades. Businesses, real estate, intellectual property, media platforms, technology systems, investment portfolios, private equity stakes, licensing agreements, audience ownership, and strategic partnerships all become components of a larger financial architecture designed to generate leverage, optionality, and recurring wealth creation opportunities.

The concept of leverage sits at the center of empire building. Wealthy capital allocators understand that time alone cannot produce extraordinary financial outcomes because individual labor capacity remains limited. Leverage allows people to multiply output beyond personal effort. Businesses create labor leverage through teams and systems. Technology creates scalability leverage through automation. Capital creates financial leverage through investments and acquisitions. Media creates influence leverage through audience reach. Intellectual property creates distribution leverage through repeatable monetization. Sophisticated entrepreneurs intentionally build multiple forms of leverage simultaneously.

One of the defining characteristics of empire builders is that they rarely rely on a single income source. Instead, they create diversified ecosystems of cash flow. Operating businesses generate active income and enterprise growth. Real estate produces recurring rental revenue and appreciation. Investments generate dividends, capital gains, and passive returns. Media assets create advertising, sponsorship, and licensing opportunities. Intellectual property generates royalties. Strategic equity stakes create future liquidity possibilities. Together, these systems reduce dependency on any one business or market condition.

The ability to allocate capital effectively becomes increasingly important as wealth grows. In the early stages of entrepreneurship, operational execution matters most because survival depends on generating revenue. But after liquidity events occur, poor capital allocation can destroy wealth surprisingly quickly. Sophisticated capital allocators evaluate opportunities based on risk-adjusted returns, scalability, cash flow potential, market trends, downside protection, and long-term strategic alignment rather than emotional excitement alone.

This is one reason why many wealthy entrepreneurs eventually build holding companies, family offices, or investment structures. These entities allow founders to centralize capital management while pursuing diversified investments strategically. Some holding companies acquire businesses directly. Others invest in startups, real estate portfolios, private equity opportunities, intellectual property, or public markets. Over time, the holding structure itself becomes a scalable financial machine independent from any single operating company.

Empire builders also understand the power of vertical integration. Rather than operating isolated businesses independently, they seek ways for companies and assets to support one another strategically. A media company may generate leads for financial services businesses. Real estate holdings may support hospitality operations. Educational platforms may feed software subscriptions. Technology infrastructure may strengthen operational efficiency across multiple companies simultaneously. Synergy creates additional leverage because the value of the ecosystem becomes greater than the sum of its individual parts.

Brand ownership plays an increasingly important role within empire building as well. Strong brands create trust, audience loyalty, pricing power, distribution advantages, and market influence. Entrepreneurs who control recognizable brands often gain easier access to partnerships, acquisitions, financing, and customer acquisition opportunities. Personal branding has become especially powerful within digital economies because audiences increasingly connect directly with founders, creators, educators, and thought leaders online.

This shift explains why many modern entrepreneurs build media platforms alongside traditional businesses. Podcasts, YouTube channels, social media audiences, newsletters, online communities, educational programs, and digital content systems create influence and audience ownership that can later support multiple monetization opportunities. Attention itself becomes an asset class.

Sophisticated capital allocators also think carefully about asymmetric opportunities. An asymmetric opportunity is one where potential upside significantly outweighs downside risk.

Venture investing often operates on this principle because a small number of successful investments may generate returns large enough to offset numerous smaller losses. Entrepreneurs who understand asymmetry allocate portions of capital toward high-upside opportunities while maintaining stable cash-flowing assets for financial resilience.

Patience becomes critically important within empire building. Many wealthy individuals create financial instability by chasing constant short-term excitement or speculative trends. Empire builders understand that compounding works most effectively across long time horizons. Businesses, investments, real estate, intellectual property, and media platforms often require years or decades to reach full value potential. Long-term ownership allows assets to appreciate while generating recurring cash flow simultaneously.

Another defining characteristic of sophisticated capital allocators is emotional discipline. Markets fluctuate constantly, industries evolve, economic cycles shift, and unexpected crises occur regularly. Entrepreneurs who react emotionally during volatility often make destructive financial decisions. Empire builders remain calm during uncertainty because they focus on long-term positioning rather than short-term noise.

The psychology of abundance also becomes increasingly important. Scarcity thinking causes many entrepreneurs to make defensive decisions rooted in fear. They hesitate to invest, overcontrol operations, or avoid delegation because they fear losing what they built. Abundance thinking recognizes that opportunities continuously emerge for adaptable individuals capable of deploying capital intelligently. This mindset encourages strategic expansion, partnerships, acquisitions, and innovation rather than defensive stagnation.

Empire building also requires learning how to attract exceptional talent. Large-scale wealth creation rarely occurs entirely alone. Sophisticated founders surround themselves with strong operators, financial experts, legal advisors, investment professionals, technologists, marketers, and strategic thinkers capable of managing complexity across multiple ventures. Human capital becomes just as important as financial capital.

The most successful empire builders eventually focus heavily on systems rather than effort alone. Systems create scalability because they continue functioning independently from constant founder involvement. Businesses with strong systems can expand across markets, teams, and industries much more effectively than businesses dependent entirely on founder labor. Systemization also increases valuation because investors prefer scalable infrastructure over personality-dependent operations. Global thinking becomes increasingly important within modern empire building as well. Digital infrastructure now allows entrepreneurs to operate internationally with unprecedented efficiency. Businesses may serve global customers, recruit remote talent, hold international investments, and diversify geographically across multiple markets simultaneously. Geographic diversification expands opportunity while reducing concentrated risk exposure.

Another important component of empire strategy involves acquiring distressed or undervalued assets during periods of market fear. Many of the largest fortunes in history were built during economic downturns when disciplined capital allocators purchased assets at discounted valuations while competitors retreated emotionally. Liquidity and patience therefore create major strategic advantages during volatile cycles.

Legacy eventually becomes central to empire thinking. Sophisticated entrepreneurs understand that true empires extend beyond personal consumption. Businesses, investments, foundations, educational systems, charitable initiatives, and family governance structures become mechanisms for creating multigenerational influence and opportunity. The goal shifts from simply becoming rich toward building structures capable of enduring long after the founder is gone. This requires long-term stewardship thinking. Wealthy families that survive multiple generations often emphasize education, responsibility, governance, and strategic discipline rather than entitlement. Empire builders recognize that preserving values matters just as much as preserving capital.

Technology continues accelerating the opportunities available to modern capital allocators. Artificial intelligence, automation, blockchain systems, digital finance, creator economies, cloud infrastructure, and global communication tools allow entrepreneurs to scale faster and broader than at any previous point in history. Individuals capable of combining technology leverage with capital allocation skill may create wealth at unprecedented speed over coming decades.

However, fundamentals still matter. Businesses must solve real problems. Customers must trust products and brands. Cash flow must eventually support sustainability. Strong governance, operational discipline, and strategic positioning remain essential regardless of technological innovation.

The transition from entrepreneur to capital allocator ultimately changes how individuals perceive opportunity itself. Operators focus primarily on immediate business execution. Capital allocators see systems, markets, networks, assets, and long-term strategic relationships. They evaluate how capital, technology, branding, ownership, and influence interact across entire ecosystems. This mindset creates exponential possibilities because the entrepreneur is no longer limited by one company, one industry, or one operational role. Capital itself becomes the tool for creating new opportunities continuously.

The future will increasingly reward individuals capable of thinking at this level. As technology reduces barriers to scalability and capital flows become more globalized, empire builders who combine operational skill with strategic capital allocation may create extraordinary long-term wealth and influence.

Ultimately, advanced capital markets strategy is not simply about building businesses. It is about constructing systems of ownership capable of compounding value across industries, generations, and economic cycles. The entrepreneur starts the engine. The capital allocator builds the empire.

The Holding Company

Victor Hale spent the first decade of his entrepreneurial life exhausted.

He owned a chain of specialty fitness centers across several states, and although the business generated millions in annual revenue, his life revolved entirely around operations. Employees called constantly. Locations required supervision. Vendors created problems. Marketing campaigns needed adjustments. Every crisis eventually reached Victor's phone.

From the outside, people considered him highly successful.

Privately, he felt trapped.

Despite strong revenue, the business consumed nearly all his time and mental energy. If Victor stopped working aggressively, growth slowed immediately. He had created income—but not freedom.

One evening, while attending a private investment conference, Victor listened to an older entrepreneur named Charles Monroe describe how he had built a multibillion-dollar holding company over several decades.

Charles explained something that permanently changed Victor's thinking.

"Most entrepreneurs stay operators forever," Charles said. "But operators trade time for scale. Capital allocators build systems that grow independently from their daily effort."

Victor became obsessed with the idea.

Over the following months, he studied holding companies, private equity structures, family offices, and long-term capital allocation strategies intensely. He realized the wealthiest individuals often did not own just one business. They owned systems of businesses, investments, intellectual property, and assets that reinforced one another strategically.

For the first time, Victor understood the difference between building a company and building an empire.

The next several years transformed his life completely.

Instead of opening additional fitness locations personally, Victor began systemizing operations aggressively. He hired experienced executives, standardized training systems, automated reporting infrastructure, and reduced operational dependence on himself. Initially, the process felt uncomfortable because he was accustomed to controlling every detail directly.

But gradually, the company became more scalable.

Then Victor made another major shift.

Instead of spending excess profits primarily on lifestyle upgrades, he began deploying capital strategically. He acquired commercial real estate beneath several gym locations. He invested in fitness technology startups, nutrition supplement brands, and online coaching platforms. He launched a media division producing fitness education content and digital memberships. At first, these investments seemed unrelated. But Victor saw something larger forming.

The gyms generated customers. The media platforms built audiences. The digital subscriptions created recurring revenue. The supplement brands increased customer monetization. The real estate appreciated independently while generating rental income.

Each asset strengthened the ecosystem.

Several years later, Victor formally created Hale Capital Holdings, a holding company structure overseeing all investments, businesses, and intellectual property assets. What once appeared to be a simple fitness business had evolved into a diversified health and wellness empire spanning media, real estate, software, licensing, supplements, and education.

The transformation accelerated rapidly.

Because Victor now operated as a capital allocator rather than purely as a gym owner, opportunities expanded exponentially. Investors approached him about partnerships. Smaller businesses requested acquisitions. Real estate developers proposed joint ventures. Media platforms sought licensing agreements.

Most importantly, Victor's time changed completely.

Instead of solving daily operational problems constantly, he focused on strategic allocation decisions. Which industries possessed long-term growth potential? Which assets generated the strongest recurring cash flow? Which acquisitions strengthened the ecosystem most effectively?

One day, during a meeting with his CFO, Victor reviewed the latest financial reports.

Surprisingly, less than half of the company's income now came directly from the original gyms.

The ecosystem itself had become larger than the founding business.

Victor smiled quietly as he realized something profound.

The gyms had never truly been the empire.

They had been the foundation.

Years later, during a private interview for a business documentary, the interviewer asked Victor what lesson transformed his wealth trajectory most significantly.

Victor answered immediately.

“I stopped thinking like a business owner,” he said. “And started thinking like a capital allocator.”

The interviewer asked him to explain further.

Victor leaned forward.

“A business owner asks, ‘How do I grow this company?’” he explained. “A capital allocator asks, ‘How do I deploy resources across systems that create compounding leverage over decades?’”

The interviewer nodded thoughtfully.

Victor continued.

“Once you understand that difference, you stop chasing income,” he said. “You start building ecosystems.”

As the cameras stopped recording, Victor looked out the office windows toward the city skyline.

Somewhere below, thousands of people were still trapped inside businesses they personally carried every day.

He understood because he had once lived exactly that way himself.

But now he saw wealth differently.

True wealth was not about working harder forever.

It was about building systems powerful enough to grow beyond you.

Chapter 10

The Billion-Dollar Framework — Scaling Beyond the Founder

The final stage of advanced capital markets strategy involves a transformation that very few entrepreneurs fully achieve. It is the transition from building a successful company into building an organization capable of operating, scaling, and compounding value independently from the founder's constant involvement. This transition separates lifestyle businesses from institutional-scale enterprises. It separates temporary success from long-term financial empires. Most importantly, it determines whether a business remains limited by the founder's personal capacity or evolves into a scalable asset capable of creating extraordinary multigenerational wealth.

At the early stages of entrepreneurship, founder dependency is often unavoidable. Founders handle sales, operations, hiring, customer service, marketing, financial management, product development, and crisis resolution simultaneously. The founder becomes the center of the business because survival requires direct involvement across nearly every function. During this stage, hard work and personal sacrifice are usually necessary. However, businesses that remain permanently dependent on founder involvement eventually reach scalability limitations. Investors, acquirers, and public markets generally place lower valuations on organizations that cannot operate effectively without the founder constantly driving execution. The reason is simple: founder dependency creates operational risk. If the founder becomes unavailable, exhausted, distracted, or unable to continue operating at the same level, the business may struggle to maintain performance.

Sophisticated entrepreneurs eventually recognize that their greatest long-term responsibility is not merely growing the company but building systems, leadership structures, and institutional infrastructure capable of scaling beyond themselves. This is the essence of the billion-dollar framework. The founder evolves from operator into architect.

An architect designs systems capable of functioning independently.

One of the first major shifts required in this transition involves abandoning the belief that the founder must personally control every important decision. Many entrepreneurs unintentionally sabotage scalability because they struggle to delegate authority effectively. They believe no one else can maintain the same quality standards, solve problems correctly, or protect the business adequately. While this mindset often comes from passion and responsibility, it eventually becomes a growth bottleneck.

The businesses that scale most successfully develop strong leadership teams capable of making high-level decisions independently. Executive infrastructure becomes critically important as organizations grow larger and more complex. Founders who recruit experienced operators, financial leaders, technology executives, legal advisors, and strategic managers increase organizational capacity dramatically.

This shift requires emotional maturity.

Many founders unconsciously tie personal identity and self-worth to being needed constantly within the business. Delegation may therefore feel psychologically threatening because it reduces founder centrality. However, scalable enterprises require systems stronger than individual personalities. Businesses that depend entirely on founder heroics rarely achieve institutional durability.

Documentation and operational systems become increasingly important as businesses scale. Institutional investors and public markets value consistency, predictability, and operational visibility. Processes must become repeatable rather than dependent on memory or improvisation. Strong systems allow companies to expand across markets, teams, geographies, and customer segments without operational chaos.

Technology infrastructure also becomes central within the billion-dollar framework. Scalable companies increasingly rely on automation, data systems, AI integration, cloud infrastructure, customer analytics, cybersecurity protocols, workflow management systems, and operational dashboards capable of supporting large-scale growth efficiently. Businesses that leverage technology strategically often achieve operating leverage far beyond traditional organizations.

Culture represents another major component of scalable enterprise design. Many entrepreneurs underestimate how culture affects long-term valuation and organizational resilience. Strong cultures align employees around shared standards, mission clarity, accountability, innovation, and customer experience. Weak cultures create internal friction, inconsistency, turnover, and operational instability.

Institutional investors evaluate leadership culture carefully because culture often determines whether companies can sustain growth under pressure. Organizations with disciplined, adaptive, high-performance cultures tend to navigate volatility more effectively than companies dependent entirely on charismatic founder leadership alone.

Scalable enterprises also require clear strategic positioning. Billion-dollar companies rarely attempt to serve everyone simultaneously. Instead, they dominate specific markets, niches, technologies, or customer categories through strong differentiation and focused execution. Strategic clarity strengthens branding, operational efficiency, customer loyalty, and investor confidence.

This is why many successful companies simplify aggressively as they scale. Complexity often destroys scalability because it increases operational friction and reduces organizational focus. Sophisticated founders learn how to identify the highest-value growth opportunities while eliminating distractions that dilute execution quality.

Data-driven decision-making becomes increasingly important as organizations expand. Smaller businesses often operate based heavily on intuition, relationships, and founder instinct. While intuition remains valuable, institutional-scale organizations require measurable systems capable of monitoring financial performance, customer behavior, operational efficiency, employee productivity, risk exposure, and strategic outcomes continuously.

Metrics create visibility.

Visibility creates control. Control increases scalability. This principle explains why institutional investors focus heavily on key performance indicators, reporting systems, margin analysis, customer acquisition costs, retention metrics, cash flow forecasting, and operational dashboards. Data reduces uncertainty, and reduced uncertainty increases valuation.

Another defining characteristic of scalable enterprises is recurring revenue stability. Investors place enormous value on predictable cash flow because it improves forecasting confidence and reduces business volatility. Subscription systems, recurring service agreements, licensing models, long-term contracts, maintenance agreements, memberships, and software platforms often command higher valuation multiples due to revenue predictability.

The billion-dollar framework also emphasizes acquisition strategy. Many highly scalable companies accelerate growth through acquisitions rather than relying solely on organic expansion. Strategic acquisitions may increase market share, strengthen technology infrastructure, eliminate competition, expand geographic reach, or improve operational capabilities rapidly.

However, acquisition-driven growth requires sophisticated integration capabilities. Poor acquisitions destroy value quickly through operational confusion, cultural conflict, excessive debt, or failed synergies. Successful acquirers build disciplined frameworks for evaluating, integrating, and scaling acquired assets strategically.

Capital structure management becomes increasingly important as organizations mature. Businesses must balance equity financing, debt financing, operational cash flow, acquisitions, and shareholder expectations intelligently. Excessive leverage may create vulnerability during downturns, while underutilized capital may limit growth opportunities. Sophisticated founders learn how to optimize capital allocation dynamically based on economic conditions and strategic objectives.

Public market readiness eventually becomes relevant for many scalable enterprises. Even companies that do not initially plan IPOs benefit from building institutional-quality governance, financial infrastructure, compliance systems, board oversight, and operational discipline because these structures increase optionality and enterprise value.

Optionality remains one of the most valuable strategic assets within the billion-dollar framework. Businesses prepared for acquisitions, IPOs, strategic partnerships, private equity recapitalizations, or long-term independent growth maintain stronger negotiating leverage and strategic flexibility. Companies trapped by one rigid pathway often lose power during changing market conditions. The relationship between scalability and founder evolution becomes increasingly important over time. Many businesses fail to scale because founders refuse to evolve personally as organizational complexity increases. The skills required to launch companies are not always the same skills required to manage institutional-scale enterprises.

Early-stage entrepreneurship rewards hustle, improvisation, and direct execution. Institutional leadership requires delegation, strategic thinking, capital allocation, governance awareness, emotional discipline, and systems design. Founders who fail to make this transition may unintentionally limit company potential despite early success.

This is why some founders eventually hire professional CEOs or transition into chairman roles while focusing on strategy, acquisitions, capital allocation, or innovation. Other founders continue leading successfully by continuously developing leadership capabilities as organizations evolve. There is no single correct structure, but scalability requires honest self-awareness regarding strengths, weaknesses, and organizational needs.

The billion-dollar framework also includes geographic and industry expansion. Scalable enterprises often move beyond single-market dependency by expanding internationally, diversifying customer bases, entering adjacent industries, or building multi-channel distribution systems. Diversification reduces concentrated risk while increasing long-term growth opportunities.

Media and influence increasingly matter within scalable enterprise strategy as well. Companies with strong public narratives, recognizable brands, loyal audiences, and thought leadership positioning often attract stronger talent, partnerships, investor interest, and customer trust. In the digital economy, attention itself becomes a strategic asset.

Another major principle involves building businesses capable of surviving the founder personally. Many entrepreneurs subconsciously build companies centered entirely around themselves. But truly institutional organizations must remain functional and valuable independent from any one individual. Succession planning, governance structures, leadership development, and operational systemization therefore become critical long-term priorities.

This principle extends into generational planning. Businesses capable of enduring across decades or generations require structures stronger than temporary leadership cycles. Some of the world's most enduring companies survived because they institutionalized culture, governance, operational excellence, and strategic discipline beyond founder identity alone. The future of scalable enterprise building will increasingly involve AI integration, automation infrastructure, decentralized operations, data intelligence, digital ecosystems, and global connectivity. However, human leadership, trust, strategic vision, and disciplined capital allocation will remain essential regardless of technological advancement.

Technology amplifies leverage, but leadership directs leverage.

Ultimately, the billion-dollar framework is not merely about reaching a specific valuation milestone. It is about creating organizations capable of scaling sustainably while preserving flexibility, resilience, operational excellence, and long-term value creation potential.

The founder who masters this transition no longer builds only a company.

They build an institution.

And institutions capable of compounding value across decades often become the foundations of extraordinary financial empires.

The Institution

Sophia Reynolds built her first company from a one-bedroom apartment with borrowed money and relentless determination.

At twenty-six years old, she launched a digital healthcare staffing platform designed to connect hospitals with remote administrative specialists and healthcare support teams. Initially, the company operated with only three employees and a handful of regional clients.

Sophia handled everything herself.

She answered customer calls, negotiated contracts, solved technical issues, managed payroll, hired employees, and worked deep into the night almost every day. During the early years, survival depended entirely on her personal effort.

The company grew steadily because hospitals desperately needed staffing flexibility and operational efficiency. Within several years, revenue expanded nationally, and investors began approaching Sophia aggressively.

Yet despite growth, the company still depended heavily on her personally.

Every important decision eventually reached her desk. Employees waited for approval constantly. Investors praised her leadership but privately questioned whether the business could truly scale institutionally.

One board member finally addressed the issue directly during a quarterly meeting.

"You built an excellent company," he told Sophia carefully. "But you haven't built an institution yet."

The comment frustrated her initially.

She believed her constant involvement protected the business. Without her oversight, mistakes might happen. Customers might become dissatisfied. Growth might slow.

But deep down, she knew the board member was right.

The company could not continue scaling indefinitely through founder intensity alone.

That realization triggered the hardest transition of Sophia's entire entrepreneurial journey.

Over the next several years, she transformed the organization systematically. She hired experienced executives from larger healthcare and technology companies. She implemented advanced operational systems, AI-driven workforce analytics, cybersecurity infrastructure, compliance frameworks, and institutional reporting systems.

Most importantly, she learned how to delegate.

The process felt emotionally uncomfortable at first. Some decisions were made differently than she would have handled them personally. Mistakes occurred occasionally. But gradually, the company became stronger because leadership capacity expanded far beyond Sophia alone.

The transformation accelerated dramatically.

Because the organization no longer depended entirely on founder involvement, acquisitions became easier to integrate. International expansion moved faster. Investors gained confidence in long-term scalability. Institutional clients signed larger contracts because operational systems appeared more sophisticated and reliable.

Then an unexpected crisis hit the industry.

A major regulatory shift disrupted healthcare staffing markets nationwide. Several competitors collapsed because their businesses lacked operational infrastructure and compliance systems strong enough to adapt quickly.

Sophia's company survived.

Not because she worked harder personally—but because the institution itself had become resilient.

The experience changed her understanding of leadership permanently. Founders often believe leadership means carrying everything personally. But institutional leadership meant designing systems capable of surviving uncertainty independently.

Years later, the company prepared for one of the largest healthcare technology IPOs of the decade.

Investment bankers praised the company's operational maturity, governance systems, recurring revenue quality, international scalability, and leadership infrastructure. Analysts repeatedly described the business as "institutional-grade."

Sophia smiled every time she heard the phrase.

Because she remembered when the company had once depended entirely on a folding table, a laptop, and endless founder exhaustion.

The IPO became massively successful.

Financial media celebrated Sophia as one of the most influential healthcare technology founders in the country. Yet privately, she understood the deeper lesson behind the success.

The valuation had not come merely from revenue growth.

It came from building an organization capable of scaling beyond herself. Several months after the IPO, Sophia spoke at a private leadership summit attended by founders from around the world. One entrepreneur asked her what separated companies that plateaued from companies that became institutions.

Sophia answered immediately.

"Founders eventually become the bottleneck if they don't evolve," she explained. "The business can only grow as large as the founder's ability to build systems stronger than personal involvement."

The room became quiet.

Sophia continued.

"Early entrepreneurship rewards hustle," she said. "But institutional scale rewards architecture."

Another founder asked what she meant by architecture.

Sophia smiled.

"Systems. Leadership. Governance. Culture. Data. Infrastructure. Scalability. Resilience," she explained. "Institutions are designed intentionally. They don't happen accidentally."

As the session ended, Sophia looked across the audience thoughtfully. Most of the founders in the room were still operating inside businesses they personally carried every day. She understood completely.

Because she had once believed that being indispensable was the goal.

Now she knew the opposite was true.

The most valuable companies in the world were the ones capable of thriving beyond the founder personally.

Final IPO Thoughts

The journey through advanced capital markets strategy ultimately leads to one central realization: the true purpose of entrepreneurship is not simply to create income, build a company, or achieve a liquidity event. The deeper purpose is to create scalable ownership systems capable of generating freedom, leverage, opportunity, and long-term wealth across multiple stages of life and business. An IPO, acquisition, recapitalization, or strategic exit is never merely a financial transaction. It is the culmination of years—sometimes decades—of vision, sacrifice, discipline, adaptation, and strategic positioning within the broader financial ecosystem.

Many entrepreneurs begin their journeys focused almost entirely on survival. In the early stages, attention centers on acquiring customers, generating revenue, managing operations, solving immediate problems, and creating stability. During these phases, it is difficult to think about capital markets, institutional investors, governance systems, or generational wealth because survival itself demands total focus. Yet the founders who eventually create extraordinary outcomes are usually those who gradually evolve their thinking beyond daily operations and begin viewing businesses as scalable financial assets capable of participating within global capital systems.

This evolution in thinking changes everything.

A founder who thinks only like an operator may build a profitable business. A founder who learns to think like a capital allocator may build an empire.

Throughout this book, one theme has appeared repeatedly: scalability drives value. Capital markets reward businesses capable of growing efficiently, generating predictable revenue, leveraging systems, reducing operational dependence on founders, and aligning with long-term economic trends. Investors do not simply buy current profits. They buy future possibility. They buy scalability, optionality, defensibility, market positioning, and confidence in future expansion.

Understanding this principle fundamentally changes how sophisticated entrepreneurs build companies. Instead of maximizing short-term extraction, they focus on increasing enterprise value. Instead of creating businesses dependent entirely on personal labor, they create systems capable of scaling independently. Instead of relying on one future outcome, they preserve strategic flexibility across multiple exit pathways. This mindset separates ordinary business ownership from advanced capital markets strategy. One of the most important lessons in modern entrepreneurship is that ownership matters more than labor alone. The modern economy increasingly rewards individuals who own scalable assets rather than those who simply sell time. Businesses, equities, intellectual property, media platforms, technology systems, real estate portfolios, and digital infrastructure all represent forms of leverage capable of compounding wealth over time. Entrepreneurs who understand ownership structures gain access to financial outcomes unavailable through labor income alone.

However, ownership without discipline can become dangerous. Many founders achieve temporary wealth only to lose it through poor capital allocation, excessive concentration risk, emotional decision-making, tax inefficiencies, or lack of long-term planning. This is why advanced capital markets strategy extends far beyond the creation of enterprise value. It also includes wealth preservation, diversification, governance, family planning, and long-term stewardship.

An IPO itself is not the finish line.

For many entrepreneurs, going public creates entirely new responsibilities and opportunities simultaneously. Public markets provide access to enormous pools of capital, increased visibility, acquisition currency, institutional credibility, and future expansion potential. But they also introduce scrutiny, volatility, governance complexity, regulatory oversight, and shareholder expectations. Founders who romanticize public markets without understanding these realities often struggle after entering them.

Sophisticated entrepreneurs recognize that liquidity events represent transitions rather than endings. The founder who successfully navigates an IPO or acquisition must eventually transform into a long-term capital allocator capable of managing wealth intelligently across decades rather than focusing only on operational execution.

This transformation becomes one of the defining shifts in long-term wealth creation.

Throughout history, some of the most successful entrepreneurs used liquidity events not as endpoints but as launching platforms for even larger opportunities. Public equity becomes acquisition currency. Capital becomes investment leverage. Media visibility becomes influence. Networks expand. Strategic optionality increases dramatically. Founders who manage these transitions intelligently often create second and third waves of wealth creation long after the original business succeeds.

Another important lesson explored throughout this book is the role of psychology within capital markets. Markets are not purely rational systems driven only by spreadsheets and financial statements. Investor sentiment, fear, greed, confidence, storytelling, narrative positioning, and public perception all influence capital flows continuously. Businesses capable of combining strong operational fundamentals with compelling long-term narratives often achieve stronger valuation outcomes than companies relying only on numbers.

Yet despite all market complexity, some principles remain timeless.

Cash flow matters.

Scalability matters.

Leadership matters.

Trust matters.

Discipline matters.

Optionality matters.

Economic cycles also remain unavoidable. Bull markets create optimism and abundant capital availability, while downturns create fear, valuation compression, and financial pressure. Entrepreneurs who survive across multiple cycles usually do so because they prioritize resilience alongside ambition. They preserve liquidity, maintain flexibility, avoid excessive fragility, and prepare for changing conditions before crises emerge.

The entrepreneurs who create lasting wealth are rarely those who simply experience one lucky market cycle. They are usually the individuals who combine long-term thinking with operational discipline and strategic adaptability across decades.

Technology is now accelerating these opportunities dramatically. Artificial intelligence, automation, cloud infrastructure, digital distribution, creator economies, and global connectivity are reducing barriers to scalability at historic speed. A single entrepreneur or small team can now build businesses capable of reaching global audiences and generating extraordinary enterprise value faster than ever before. The future will increasingly reward individuals capable of combining technological leverage with financial intelligence and strategic capital allocation.

But technology alone does not guarantee success.

The future still belongs to entrepreneurs who solve meaningful problems, create genuine value, build trust, and operate with long-term vision. Markets eventually punish hype without substance. Sustainable wealth creation still depends on fundamentals even as technology changes the tools used to build businesses.

One of the greatest dangers entrepreneurs face after achieving success is complacency. Markets evolve constantly. Industries transform. Competitive landscapes shift rapidly. The founder who stops learning eventually becomes vulnerable. Lifelong adaptability therefore becomes essential within advanced capital markets strategy. Entrepreneurs who remain curious, flexible, and strategically aware often maintain relevance across multiple generations of innovation and economic change.

Legacy eventually becomes the deeper question behind all wealth creation.

Most founders initially pursue entrepreneurship for freedom, financial security, or independence. Over time, however, many begin asking larger questions about impact, family continuity, philanthropy, education, mentorship, and long-term contribution. Wealth itself eventually becomes less meaningful without purpose attached to it.

This is why some of the most sophisticated entrepreneurs build family offices, charitable foundations, educational initiatives, investment platforms, and multigenerational governance systems designed to create lasting influence beyond personal consumption. Businesses may generate capital, but legacy determines how that capital shapes future lives and opportunities.

The modern economy offers extraordinary possibilities for founders willing to think strategically. Entrepreneurs no longer need enormous industrial infrastructure to create scalable global enterprises. Digital systems, automation, intellectual property, media platforms, and AI-driven technologies have dramatically expanded what individuals can accomplish with relatively lean operational structures.

At the same time, competition has intensified globally. Information moves instantly. Markets evolve rapidly. Capital flows internationally. This means entrepreneurs must become increasingly sophisticated not only operationally but financially and strategically as well.

The founders who dominate future capital markets will likely possess several defining characteristics:

They will think long term while acting decisively.

They will build systems instead of depending entirely on personal labor.

They will understand technology without becoming blindly dependent on trends.

They will preserve optionality rather than becoming trapped by rigid plans.

They will prioritize ownership and leverage over status and consumption.

They will combine operational excellence with strategic capital allocation.

They will understand that true wealth is built through compounding across time rather than chasing short-term excitement.

Perhaps most importantly, they will recognize that entrepreneurship is not simply about making money. It is about building scalable systems capable of creating freedom, opportunity, resilience, and impact far beyond the founder personally.

Every major business begins with uncertainty. No entrepreneur can predict every market cycle, technological shift, investor reaction, or economic disruption. Yet despite uncertainty, disciplined founders continue building because they understand one essential truth: ownership creates possibility.

The business you build today may become tomorrow's acquisition target, public company, investment platform, media ecosystem, or multigenerational family enterprise. The systems you create now may generate opportunities far larger than you currently imagine possible. The habits, relationships, operational discipline, and strategic thinking you develop throughout the entrepreneurial journey often become more valuable than any single transaction itself.

This is why advanced capital markets strategy matters.

It teaches entrepreneurs how to move beyond survival thinking into strategic ownership thinking. It teaches founders how to align businesses with scalability, investor psychology, market timing, institutional capital, and long-term wealth preservation. It transforms entrepreneurship from isolated business building into comprehensive financial architecture design.

Ultimately, the IPO is not the dream.

The dream is freedom.

The dream is optionality.

The dream is ownership.

The dream is creating systems so valuable and scalable that they continue generating opportunity long after the founder steps away from daily operations.

The dream is building something capable of outlasting economic cycles, technological shifts, and even generations themselves.

And for the entrepreneurs willing to think at that level, the possibilities remain almost limitless.

www.ingramcontent.com/pod-product-compliance
Ingram Content Group UK Ltd.
Pitfield, Milton Keynes, MK11 3LW, UK
UKHW010011031026
15589UKWH00008B/1596

9 798256 015916